Linguistic Resources for Automatic Natural Language Generation (LiRA@NLG 2017)

Santiago de Compostela, Spain
4 September 2017

Editors:

Kristina Kocijan
Peter Machonis
Max Silberztein

ISBN: 978-1-5108-4758-3

Printed from e-media with permission by:

Curran Associates, Inc.
57 Morehouse Lane
Red Hook, NY 12571

Some format issues inherent in the e-media version may also appear in this print version.

Printed by Curran Associates, Inc. (2017)

Association for Computational Linguistics
209 N. Eighth Street
Stroudsburg, Pennsylvania 18360

Phone: 1-570-476-8006
Fax: 1-570-476-0860

acl@aclweb.org

Additional copies of this publication are available from:

Curran Associates, Inc.
57 Morehouse Lane
Red Hook, NY 12571 USA
Phone: 845-758-0400
Fax: 845-758-2633
Email: curran@proceedings.com
Web: www.proceedings.com

LiRA@NLG 2017

Proceedings of the Linguistic Resources for Automatic Natural Language Generation Workshop

Santiago de Compostela, Spain

September 4, 2017

Edited by Kristina Kocijan, Peter Machonis & Max Silberztein

Preface

The Linguistic Resources for Automatic Natural Language Generation (LiRA@NLG) workshop of the International Natural Language Generation INLG2017 Conference held at Santiago de Compostela, September 4, 2017, brought together participants involved in developing large-coverage linguistic resources and researchers with an interest in expanding real-world Natural Language Generation (NLG) software.

Linguists and developers of NLG software have been working separately for many years: NLG researchers are typically more focused on technical issues specific to text generation—where good performance (e.g. recall and precision) is crucial—whereas linguists tend to focus on problems related to the development of exhaustive and precise resources that are mainly 'neutral' vis-a-vis any NLP application (e.g. parsing or generating sentences), using various grammatical formalisms such as NooJ, TAG or HPSG. However, recent progress in both fields is reducing many of these differences, with large-coverage linguistic resources being more and more used by robust NLP software. For instance, NLG researchers can now use large dictionaries of multiword units and expressions, and several linguistic experiments have shown the feasibility of using large phrase-structure grammars (a priori used for text parsing) in 'generation' mode to automatically produce paraphrases of sentences that are described by these grammars. The eight papers presented at the LiRA@NLG workshop focused on the following questions:

- How do we develop 'neutral' linguistic resources (dictionaries, morphological, phrase-structure and transformational grammars) that can be used both to parse and generate texts automatically?

- Is it possible to generate grammatical sentences by using linguistic data alone, i.e. with no statistical methods to remove ambiguities? What are the limitations of rule-based systems, as opposed to stochastic ones?

The common themes that these articles explore are: how to build large-coverage dictionaries and morphological grammars that can be used by NLG applications, how to integrate a linguistically-based Generation module into a Machine-Translation system, and how to construct a syntactic grammar that can be used by a transformational engine to perform paraphrase generation. Linguists as well as Computational Linguists who work on Automatic Generation based on linguistic methods will find advanced, up-to-the-minute studies on these topics in this volume:

- Max Silberztein's article, "Automatic Generation from FOAF to English: Linguistic Contribution to Web Semantics," presents an automatic system capable of generating a large number of English sentences from *Friend Of A Friend* (FOAF) statements in the RDF Turtle notation using NooJ's transformational engine both in Parse and Generation modes.

- Silvia García Méndez, Milagros Fernández Gavilanes, Enrique Costa Montenegro, Jonathan Juncal Martínez and Francisco Javier González Castaño's paper, "Lexicon for Natural Language Generation in Spanish Adapted to Alternative and Augmentative Communication," introduces *Elsa*, the first lexicon for Spanish automatically generated from a pictogram resource and tailored for Augmentative and Alternative Communication (AAC).

- Essia Bessaies, Slim Mesfar and Henda Ben Ghezala's study, "Generating Answering Patterns from Factoid Arabic Questions," presents the module that generates answers in Arabic for factoid questions, in an automatic Question Answering system.

- Kristina Kocijan, Božo Bekavac and Krešimir Šojat's contribution, "Language Generation from DB Query," demonstrates how to produce short textual summary written in Croatian from the pieces of data found in databases in the domain of airline tickets.

- Peter Machonis' article, "Using Electronic Dictionaries and NooJ to Generate Sentences Containing English Phrasal Verbs," illustrates a method for generating English sentences that contain phrasal verbs; the main difficulty is due to the fact that phrasal verbs are discontinuous.

- Hela Fehri and Sondes Dardour's study, "Generating Text with Correct Verb Conjugation: Proposal for a New Automatic Conjugator with NooJ," presents an automatic system capable of generating verbs conjugated forms in three languages: Arabic, French and English.

- Jouda Ghorbel's paper, "Formalization of Speech Verbs with NooJ for Machine Translation: the French Verb *accuser*," shows how to disambiguate French verbs (taking the verb *accuser* as an example) and generate the appropriate, exact translation into Arabic.

- Ikram Bououd and Rania Fafi's paper, "Using Serious Games to Correct French Dictations: Proposal for a New Unity3D/NooJ Connector," presents a system that generates written text from a vocal input, which can be used to help students learn French as a second language.

It is worth noting that several participants are using the NooJ software to develop the large-coverage linguistic resources needed by their NLG applications. We think that readers will appreciate the importance of this volume, both for the intrinsic value of each linguistic formalization and the underlying methodology, as well as for the potential for developing Automatic Generation applications.

Kristina Kocijan
Peter Machonis
Max Silberztein

Organizing Committee

Kristina Kocijan, University of Zagreb, Croatia

Peter Machonis, Florida International University, USA

Max Silberztein, Université de Franche-Comté, France

Scientific Committee

Héla Fehri, University of Gabes, Tunisia

Yuras Hetsevich, United Institute of Informatic Problems, Belarus

Kristina Kocijan, University of Zagreb, Croatia

Elena Lloret Pastor, Universidad de Alicante, Spain

Peter Machonis, Florida International University, USA

Slim Mesfar, University of Carthage, Tunisia

Simon Mille, Universitat Pompeu Fabra, Spain

Max Silberztein, Université de Franche-Comté, France

Table of Contents

Automatic Generation from FOAF to English: Linguistic Contribution to Web Semantics

Max Silberztein *1*

Lexicon for Natural Language Generation in Spanish Adapted to Alternative and Augmentative Communication

Silvia García Méndez, Milagros Fernández Gavilanes, Enrique Costa Montenegro, Jonathan Juncal Martínez and Francisco Javier González Castaño *11*

Generating Answering Patterns from Factoid Arabic Questions

Essia Bessaies, Slim Mesfar and Henda Ben Ghezala *17*

Language Generation from DB Query

Kristina Kocijan, Božo Bekavac and Krešimir Šojat *25*

Using Electronic Dictionaries and NooJ to Generate Sentences Containing English Phrasal Verbs

Peter Machonis *33*

Generating Text with Correct Verb Conjugation: Proposal for a New Automatic Conjugator with NooJ

Hela Fehri and Sondes Dardour *39*

Formalization of Speech Verbs with NooJ for Machine Translation: the French Verb *accuser*

Jouda Ghorbel *43*

Using Serious Games to Correct French Dictations: Proposal for a New Unity3D/NooJ Connector

Ikram Bououd and Rania Fafi *49*

From FOAF to English: Linguistic Contribution to Web Semantics

Max Silberztein
Université de Franche-Comté
max.silberztein@univ-fcomte.fr

Abstract

This paper presents a linguistic module capable of generating a set of English sentences that correspond to a Resource Description Framework (RDF) statement; I discuss how a generator can control the linguistic module, as well as the various limitations of a pure linguistic framework.

1 Introduction

Automatic Natural Language Generation Software aims to express information stored in a knowledge database as a Natural Language text. The information at the source typically consists of a series of simple atomic statements, such as "John owns a house", "Mary lives in Manchester", "Peter is Ann's cousin". These statements are usually stored in a knowledge database or ontology in a formal notation such as Prolog (e.g. "Own(John,House)") or XML.

Translating each elementary statement into an isolated English sentence is straightforward; the difficulty arises when one tries to process a complex set of statements to generate a text that feels "natural": an entity that is mentioned several times might then have to be referred to by a pronoun, a possessive determiner (e.g. *He is her cousin*), or an anaphoric term (e.g. *The student is her cousin*); a complement might need to be brought into focus (e.g. *It is Peter who is Ann's cousin*); subsequent sentences might need to agree in tense and aspect, etc. For each original individual statement, there might be thousands of potential English sentences that can express it: the generator must then decide which sentence to produce. This article presents the linguistic component of such a system.

2 The linguistic framework

Based on the principles of linguistic approaches to generation laid out by Danlos (1987), I have used the NooJ[1] platform to construct a set of linguistic resources that parses a sequence of RDF statements and produces a corresponding set of English sentences. NooJ allows linguists to construct structured sets of linguistic resources ("modules") in the form of dictionaries and grammars[2] to formalize a large gamut of linguistic phenomena: orthography and spelling, inflectional, derivational and agglutinative morphology, local and structural syntax, transformational syntax, lexical and predicative semantics. All linguistic analyses are performed sequentially by adding and/or removing linguistic annotations to/from a Text Annotation Structure (TAS); at each level of the analysis, each parser uses the annotations that were added to the TAS by preceding parsers, and then adds new annotations to the TAS, or deletes annotations that have been proven to be incorrect. This architecture allows the system to perform complex linguistic operations that require information coming from all levels of analyses, even when total disambiguation was not possible at earlier stages of the analysis, thus avoiding the problems at the heart of criticisms against pure linguistic approaches.[3]

For instance, to generate the sentence "She is Joe's love" from the elementary statement "Joe loves Lea", a linguistic system needs to access the following information:

[1] See Silberztein (2016a). NooJ is a free, open-source linguistic development environment supported by the European Metashare program.

[2] Regular Grammars, Context-Free Grammars, Context-Sensitive Grammars and Unrestricted Grammars can be entered either in a textual or in a graphical form. The grammars shown in this article are graphical Context-Sensitive Grammars.

[3] See for instance the "generation gap" discussed by Gardent Perez-Beltrachini (2017).

Proceedings of the Linguistic Resources for Automatic Natural Language Generation Workshop, pages 1–9, Santiago de Compostela, Spain, September 4, 2017.

- the word "loves" can be a conjugated form of lexical entry *to love*;[4]
- the verb *to love* can be nominalized into the Human Noun *a love*;[5]
- the structure N_0 V N_1 can be restructured as N_1 is N_0's V-n;
- the Noun *Lea* is feminine therefore it can be replaced with pronoun *she* when it is in a subject position.

One important characteristic of NooJ resources is that they are "application-neutral": they can be used both by parsers and by generators. This allows a single software application to both:

- parse sentences, e.g., from sentence "*It is not Lea that he loves*", produce the analysis "*Joe loves Lea* +Focus1 +Neg +Pron1",
- or, the other way around, given the elementary sentence "*Joe loves Lea*" and the series of operators "+Pro0 +Preterit +AspCont +Intens2", generate the complex sentence "*He continued to love Lea for a long time*".

Given the elementary sentence *Joe loves Lea*, Silberztein (2016b) showed that by combining linguistic operations such as negation (e.g. *Joe does not love Lea*), focus (e.g. *It is Joe who loves Lea*), tense (e.g. *Joe loved Lea*), aspect (e.g. *Joe has stopped loving Lea*), modality (e.g. *Joe should love Lea*), intensity (e.g. *Joe loves Lea passionately*), pronominalization (e.g. *He loves her*), nominalization (e.g. *Joe is in love with Lea*), etc., a system can generate over a million declarative sentences (e.g. *It is not her that he stopped loving*), about 500,000 nominal phrases (e.g. *Joe's passionate love for her*) and over 3 million questions (e.g. *When did Joe start loving her?*). Each generated sentence is associated with the series of transformations (e.g. +Passive, +Focus1) used to produce it.

In this article, I show how this system can be adapted so that an NLG system can control what exact English sentence(s) need to be generated.

3 FOAF Predicates

The Semantic Web[6] constitutes a gigantic network of ontologies that contain elementary pieces of information, written in the RDF syntax. A typical RDF statement is a triple that contains one subject entity, one predicate and one object entity; the predicate states the type of relationship between the two entities. All three elements are identified by a URI. For instance, the following RDF triple states that the person "Mark_Twain" is the author of the book "Huckleberry_Fin":[7]

```
<http://example.org/Mark_Twain>
<http://example.org/author>
<http://example.org/Huckleberry_Fin>.
```

In this article, I focus on the *Friend Of A Friend* (FOAF) ontology (FOAF Vocabulary Specification 2010), which contains a set of classes for entities:

Agent, Document, Group, Image, Organization, Person, Project...

and a set of properties (i.e. predicates), e.g.:

account, age, based near, birthday, currentProject, familyName, gender, givenName, interest, knows, name, title...

4 From RDF to English

A linguistic module capable of parsing RDF statements and producing the corresponding potential English sentences needs the following resources:

- a set of lexical and morphological resources to link all words and expressions to their actual inflected and derived forms (I am using NooJ's default English module);
- a syntactic grammar to parse an RDF statement and extract from it the value of its entities and predicate;
- one syntactic grammar for each FOAF property, in order to describe the set of English sentences that can be used to express it.

The grammar for FOAF property *currentProject* shown in Figure 1 contains four parts:

- **Turtle**: this grammar describes RDF statements expressed in the simple Turtle notation;

[4] There are other possible analyses such as in *loves* = Plural of Noun *a love*.

[5] There is a second nominalization that is not in play here : *Joe's love for Lea*, where *love* is an abstract noun.

[6] See Berners-Lee et al. (2001).

[7] I am using the Terse RDF Triple Language (Turtle) syntax, see RDF1.1. Turtle (2014).

- **declarative**, this grammar describes declarative sentences, e.g. *Tim Berners-Lee is currently working on the World Wide Web project*
- **noun phrase** describes noun phrases, e.g. *Tim Berners-Lee's World Wide Web current project*
- **question** describes questions, e.g. *Is Tim Berners-Lee involved in the World Wide Web project?*

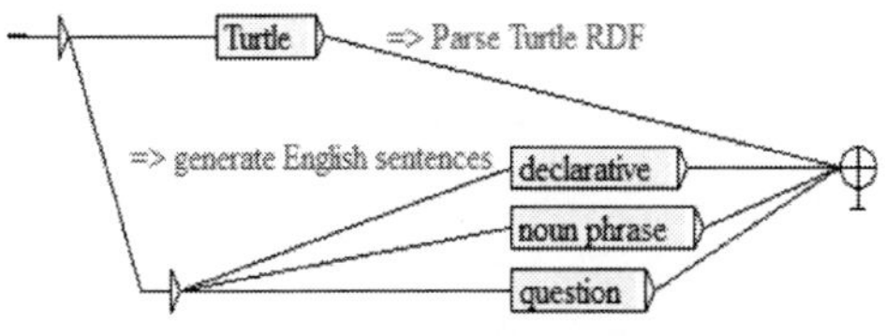

Figure 1: Parse RDF and generate sentences

Note that the same grammar can be used to parse an RDF statement and produce the corresponding English equivalent (sentences, phrases and questions), or reciprocally, to parse any English sentence, phrase or question and produce the corresponding RDF statement. In this article, I assume that the system receives an RDF statement as its input; it will then produce the corresponding English declarative sentences, phrases and questions.

4.1 Parsing an RDF statement

Parsing an RDF statement written in the simplified Turtle notation is straightforward: a statement is a sequence of three XML tags followed by a period; each tag contains an URI that represents an entity or a predicate. For instance, consider the following triple:

```
<http://dbpedia.org/Tim_Berners-Lee>
<http://xmlns.com/foaf/0.1/currentProject>
<http://dbpedia.org/World_Wide_Web>.
```

Grammar **XML**, shown in Figure 2, extracts the suffix of each tag's URI and stores it in variable **$Suf**. Note that the suffix may contain any number of letters, digits, periods, dashes and underscore characters.[8]

The main grammar **Turtle** shown in Figure 3 contains three references to the **XML** graph: it parses a sequence of three consecutive XML tags and computes the value of each variable **$Suf**. Each subsequent value of **$Suf** is then copied to the corresponding global variables **@Subject**, **@Predicate** and **@Object**.[9]

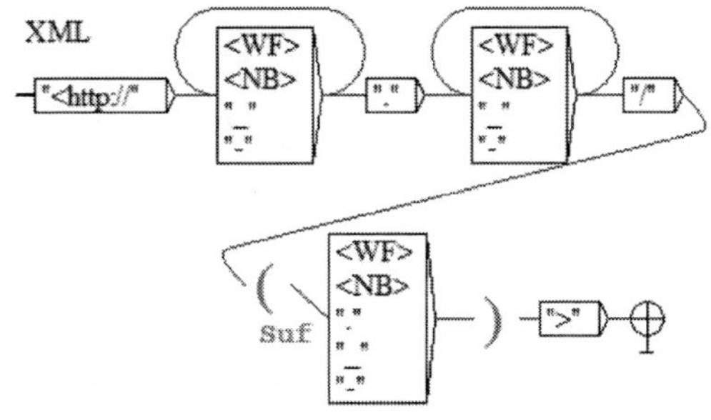

Figure 2: Parse XML tags

After parsing the previous RDF statement, variable **@Subject** is set to "Tim_Berners-Lee", variable **@Predicate** is set to "currentProject" and variable **@Object** is set to "World_Wide_Web".

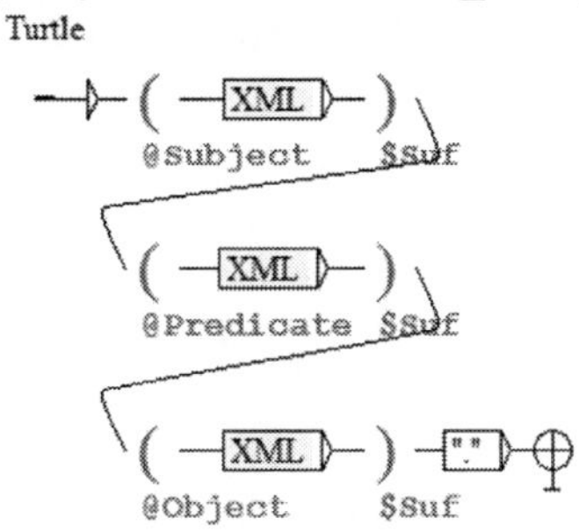

Figure 3: Parsing Turtle RDF Statements

4.2 Generating English Sentences

Each property from the FOAF ontology corresponds to a set of English sentences that can be used to express it. In this approach, one must construct one grammar to generate all the English sentences that correspond to each of the FOAF properties *name*, *firstName*, *givenName* and *familyName* (e.g. *His first name is Tim, Berners-Lee's given name is Tim*), a grammar that corresponds to the FOAF property *age* (e.g. *John is 18-month old; Mary is 12; Joe is still a teenager; Lea is a senior citizen*), a grammar that expresses the fact that a person knows another person (e.g. *John is acquainted with Mary, Lea has met Joe already*), a grammar that expresses the fact that a person is currently working on a project, another for

[8] <WF> matches any sequence of letters; <NB> matches any sequence of digits.

[9] Variables with prefix "@" have a global scope. This allows the system to link a given entity to all its references (e.g. "Lea" with Pronoun "her") across a grammar that may contain dozens of graphs. Here, we want to link **@Predicate** to all its English corresponding terms, whether they are Verbs (e.g. *works on*), Adjectives (*is involved in*) or even Nouns (e.g. *head of*).

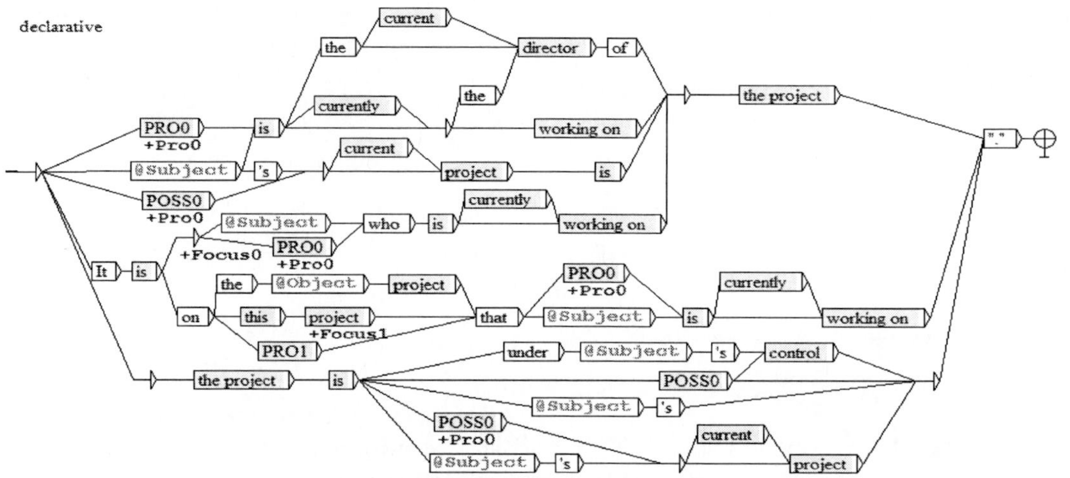

Figure 4: Declarative Sentences

property *pastProject*, another for property *enemyOf*, etc.

Being able to automatically produce questions would be useful for a few specialized applications such as literature or language teaching (whereas a software automatically generates questions from a study text that students are expected to answer) or question answering, whereas sentences recognized by the **declarative** grammar are potential answers for any question recognized by the **question** grammar.[10] In this article, I present the **declarative** and **noun phrase** grammars.

4.3 Declarative Sentences

The entrance point for the grammar that represents (i.e. can parse and/or generate) the declarative sentences for property *currentProject* is shown in Figure 4.

The grammar uses the value of the variables **@Subject** and **@Object** (in red in the graph) that were set by the parsing of the *currentProject* RDF statement. This graph contains references to embedded graphs (in yellow in the graph) such as **current, project, the project**, etc. For instance, the embedded grammar **current** represents the following Adjectives:

- **current** = current | in progress | ongoing | present | present-day;

The grammar **project** contains the following nouns:

- **project** = activity | affair | adventure | assignment | business | creation | enterprise | job | project | scheme | task | venture;

The graph for **the project** is displayed in Figure 5.

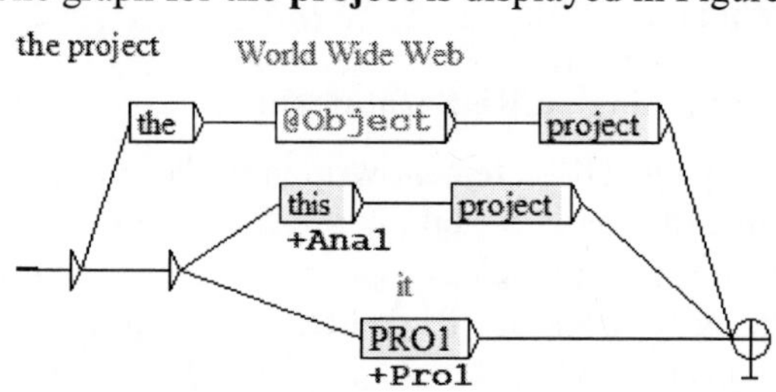

Figure 5: Graph for "the project"

Note that this graph can produce anaphoric terms as well as pronouns, e.g.:

> *Tim Berners-Lee is currently working on* **that enterprise. It** *is under Tim Berners-Lee's control.*

The **declarative** grammar for property *currentProject* contains over 30 graphs and represents (i.e. can both parse or generate) over 50,000 declarative sentences.

[10] The **question** grammar generates over one million questions, such as *Who is working on the World Wide Web project? What is Tim Berners-Lee's current project? Is Tim Berners-Lee involved in the World Wide Web project?*

4.4 Noun Phrases

The entrance point for the grammar that represents the noun phrases that might be used to express property *currentProject* can be seen in Figure 6.

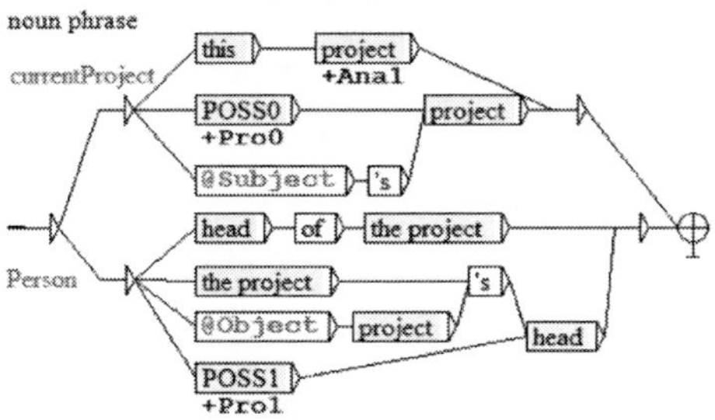

Figure 6: Noun Phrases

This grammar represents (i.e. parses or generates) two types of noun phrases: phrases that focus on the *currentProject* entity, e.g.:

> *Tim Berner-Lee's World Wide Web, his ongoing project, etc.*

and phrases that focus on the *person* entity, e.g.:

> *The World Wide Web project's current director, the present head of that enterprise, its director, etc.*

This grammar does not describe phrases that focus on the date (e.g. *the moment when Tim Berners-Lee's project is the World Wide Web*), even though the information that the project is "current" is a crucial part of the information represented by the RDF statement. Generating phrases from RDF statements that explicitly refer to a project's initial and/or ending dates will require other grammars for dates, such as the default one available in the NooJ's English module.

5 Pronouns and anaphora

The grammar *currentProject* produces certain sentences and phrases that should not be generated in isolation, e.g.:

> *He is currently involved in that project. His project.*

If the goal is to produce one isolated sentence or phrase, that sentence or phrase should not contain any pronoun, possessive determiner or anaphoric term, otherwise the original information would be lost. However, most NLG applications aim at producing texts that are sequences of related sentences and phrases: in order to keep the resulting text natural, it is then important to be able to use pronouns, possessive determiners, anaphoric terms, as well as every linguistic operator the language offers: aspect, derivation, focus, intensity, modality, tense, etc.[11]

6 Aspect and Tense

The *currentProject* property limits the possible aspect and tense of the generated English sentences to present or present progressive: the linguistic module generates sentences such as the following ones:

> *Tim Berners-Lee (works | is working | is currently working) on the World Wide Web project; Tim Berners-Lee (is involved | is currently involved) in the World Wide Web project; Tim Berners-Lee's (current | in progress | on going | present | present-day) project is the World Wide Web project,* etc.

but it may also generate sentences such as the following ones:

> [+Tense]: *Tim Berners-Lee (was working | has worked | will be working) on the World Wide Web project.*
>
> [+Aspect]: *Tim Berners-Lee started working on the World Wide Web project (in 1989); Tim Berners-Lee has been working on the World Wide Web (for 20 years); Tim Berners-Lee will stop working on the World Wide Web (next year).*
>
> [+Modality]: *Tim Berners-Lee should work on the World Wide Web project; Tim Berners-Lee can work on the World Wide Web; Tim Berners-Lee might work on the World Wide Web.*

as well as sentences that contain any combination of Tense / Aspect / Modality variants:

> *Tim Berners-Lee could have started to work on the WWW project (one year earlier). Steve Jobs has worked on the iPhone project (for a long time). Jürgen E. Schrempp initiated the Chrysler-Daimler merger task (last year). Has Larry Page been involved in the Alphabet Inc.*

[11] See Lloret Pastor (2011) on how the COMPENDIUM automatic summary system manages redundancy and information fusion. The WebNLG Challenge also aims at producing a sequence of sentences that might contain elisions, anaphora or pronouns.

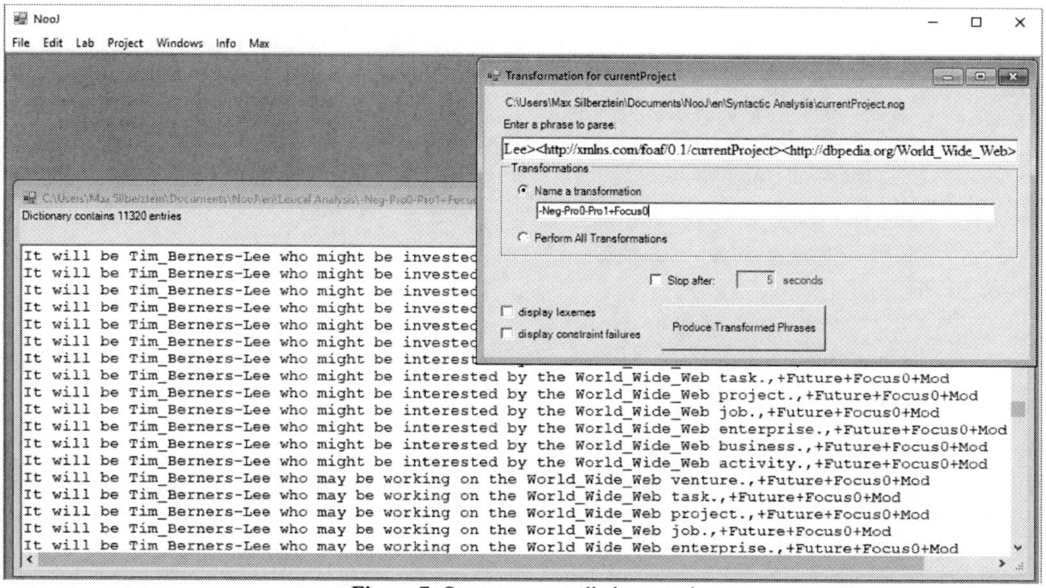

Figure 7: Operator-controlled generation

Company adventure (from the very beginning)?

Based on the sole *currentProject* property, it might not be appropriate to generate these sentences; however, text generators are always used to express more than one piece of information; these sentences will be useful if the generator needs to produce sentences that express properties such as *pastProject*, or if the generator has access to date information such as: *when did Tim Berners-Lee start to work on the WWW*, *when does Jürgen E. Schremp plan to stop working on the merger*, *how long has Larry Page been working on the creation of the Alphabet Inc. Company?* etc.

The linguistic module cannot perform extra-linguistic computations, such as producing complements such as *for 28 years* by subtracting the initial project's date from the current date, by itself. It can, however, perform simple equality tests by using constraints such as <$gender="Male"> (to pronominalize *Tim Berners-Lee* as *he*), and <$pastProject=$currentProject> (to produce sentences such as *Tim Berners-Lee is still working on the World Wide Web*).

7 Controlling the linguistic module

To control what sentence is to be generated, the generator that pilots the linguistic system must send a set of operators that act as parameters. Following are examples of sentences generated, given a set of operators:

- [+AspTilNow+Pro0+Focus1]:
  It is on the World Wide Web venture that he has been working until now.
- [+When+Preterit+Pro0+Pro1]:
  When did he work on that enterprise?
- [+Neg+Future+AspStop]:
  Tim Berners-Lee will no longer work on the World Wide Web adventure.

Operators can be sent to the linguistic module with a "+" or a "-" prefix, to control whether the generator wants to activate, or filter out, the corresponding sentences and phrases. For instance, the generator may filter out sentences that contain a negation or a pronoun with the following sequence of operators: [-Neg-Pro0-Pro1]. Figure 7 shows that this exact sequence of operators makes the linguistic system produce over 11,000 declarative sentences, none of which include a negation or a pronoun.

7.1 Incorrect information

One problem with the pure linguistic approach is that, if not properly controlled, the linguistic module will also generate sentences that misrepresent the initial FOAF information, e.g.:

- [+Neg]:
  Tim Berners-Lee is not currently working on the World Wide Web project
- [+Future+AspCont+Intens2]:
  Tim Berners-Lee will keep on working on the World Wide Web project forever

However, even though the previous sentences are not appropriate, some combinations of these operators may produce correct statements, e.g.:

- [+Neg+Future+AspCont+Intens2]:
  Tim Berners-Lee will not keep on working on the World Wide Web project forever

In other words, linguistic operators such as +Neg or +Future are not "bad" intrinsically: they must be controlled by the generator, just like any other linguistic operator: it is the responsibility of the calling application (here, the generator) to control the linguistic module by setting the correct parameters in order to enable or disable the production of each sentence and phrase.

8 Limitations

There are a few problems with the prototype as it is now.

8.1 Missing information

The single FOAF statement that constitutes the input of the linguistic prototype presented in this article does not mention the entities' names. Therefore, the sentences generated by the prototype actually resemble the following:

Tim_Berners-Lee is currently working on the World_Wide_Web project.

In a finalized software application, the generator should retrieve the value of the person's name property, available as an FOAF property:

```
<foaf:name xml:lang="en"> Tim Berners-Lee </foaf:name>
```

Using the value of the FOAF *givenName*, *firstName* and *familyName* properties for *person* entities would allow the linguistic component to generate abbreviated variants such as "Berners-Lee", or even "Tim" (in a casual context, for instance). In the same manner, the linguistic module would need to access a list of variants and abbreviations for each *project* entity, such as "the Web" or "WWW" for entity World_Wide_Web.

Another important piece of information is the gender of each *person* entity: for Tim_Berners-Lee, the generator needs to combine operator +Pro0 with operator +Mas to stop the linguistic module from generating incorrect feminine or neutral pronouns or possessive determiners such as in: *The World Wide Web is (her | its) current project.*[12] As this information is available in FOAF:

```
<foaf:gender xml:lang="en">Male</foaf:gender>
```

Another possibility is to add this FOAF statement to the linguistic module to its input, store the value of the gender in a variable (e.g. $gender), and add a constraint on the variable in the grammar everywhere we need to produce a pronoun, such as in Figure 8.

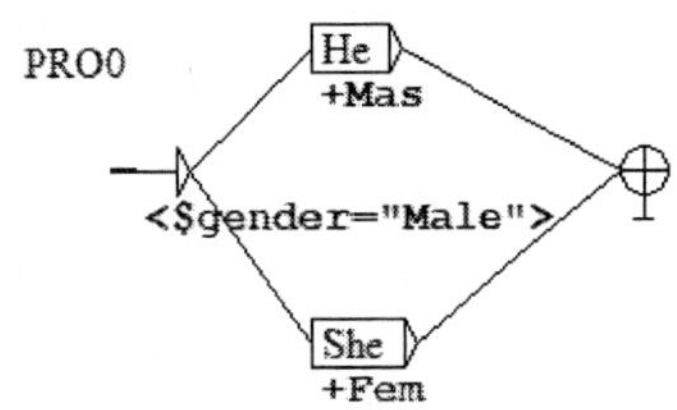

Figure 8: Adding gender information

8.2 What is a *project*?

Because the Web Semantics' entities are meant to represent elements of meanings independent from the languages, they tend to be more generic than actual English terms, which makes it difficult to compute back the sets of English terms they represent.[13]

For instance, the FOAF *project* class regroups entities that are not always easily referred to by the English term "project": it makes sense to qualify the World Wide Web as a project, an enterprise or even a program, but it is much more difficult to use the following terms:

Tim Berners-Lee is currently working on the World Wide Web (activity | affair | assignment | business | creation | job | management | scheme | task | venture)

---

[12] *gender* is an FOAF property attached to class Agent rather than its subclass *Person*. The generator will therefore need to make entity Tim_Berners-Lee inherit its gender property to make it explicit to the linguistic module.

[13] The vagueness and inconsistency of the Semantic Web are its two most common criticisms.

The World Wide Web has existed too long to be qualified as an *affair*; it is too big to be qualified as a *task*; it is not an *assignment*, nor a *business*, Tim Berners-Lee does not "manage" it, etc.

However, these terms would be more appropriate for other *currentProject* entities, e.g.:

> *Larry Page is responsible for the Alphabet Inc. Company (adventure | affair | business | creation | task | venture)*

Other FOAF classes such as *Group* and *Organization* might be relevant for describing what the World Wide Web or the Alphabet Inc. Company are: having the information that the World Wide Web is both a *project* and an *organization* will allow the linguistic module to produce much better sentences.

8.3 What does the *person* do exactly?

A similar problem concerns the *person* entity: when a project is described in FOAF as someone's current project, it is not clear what this person does, exactly: Is Tim Berners-Lee the *originator,* or the *creator*, or the *inventor* of the Web? Is Steve Jobs the *designer*, or the *mastermind*, or the *leader* of the iPhone project? Is Larry Page the *founder*, or the *originator*, or the *father* of the Alphabet Inc. Company? Is *Jürgen E. Schrempp* the *artisan*, or the *architect*, or the *facilitator* of the Mercedes-Chrysler merger? Even though both the *person* and the *project* entities are well defined, at this point we do not have the capability to select which exact terms can be used naturally: therefore, at this point, the linguistic prototype produces a large number of not-so-natural phrases such as "the World Wide Web task" or "the iPhone affair".

8.4 How current is a currentProject?

When a project is described in FOAF as a *currentProject*, it is not clear whether it is possible or not to replace the prototypic adverb *currently* with expressions such as: *for the moment, right now, these days*, etc., and if tenses other than present or present progressive (such as present perfect or future) are adequate or not:

- [+PresentPerfect]:
  Tim Berners-Lee has worked on the World Wide Web project (OK)
- [+PresentPerfect+AspCont+Intens1]:
  Tim Berners-Lee has been working on the World Wide Web project for a long time (OK)
- [+Future]:
  Tim Berners-Lee will work on the World Wide Web project (not OK)
- [+Future+AspCont+Intens1]:
  Tim Berners-Lee will continue to work on the World Wide Web project for a long time (not OK)

It will be necessary to explore the FOAF ontology to check if the *currentProject* is also listed as a *pastProject*; if so, the generator can send the operators +AspCont and +PresentPerfect to the linguistic module. The more information the generator has access to, the more it will be able to generate sentences produced by the linguistic module. As of now, unfortunately, we need to restrict the generation capability of the linguistic module drastically: the system is far from producing most of the English sentences that occur on the Web, such as the following ones:

> *Under Jobs' exacting leadership, Apple pioneered many things with the iPhone. Tim Berners-Lee is the director of the World Wide Web Consortium. Larry Page: I am really excited to be running Alphabet as CEO with help from my capable partner, Sergey, as President.*

However, grammars developed with NooJ are meant to be used not only for the generation, but also for the parsing of any text, including the previous sentences: the fact that a large number of sentences generated by the linguistic module are not yet useable by the generator is a consequence of the extreme simplicity of the FOAF ontology, rather than of a shortcoming of linguistics.

9 Conclusion

It is possible to construct a system capable of translating RDF statements into a rich set of English sentences. As a generator taps into the power of expression of the English language, it needs to control it: this can be performed via the use of linguistic operators.

Some operators, such as +Focus0 or +Pro1, are "information neutral", in the sense that they do not produce English sentences that might betray the information of the original RDF statement: they are typically used for rhetorical purposes, to make the resulting text more natural.

Other linguistic operators, such as +Neg, +Future or +AspCont, are more "dangerous" to use, but should be easy to control, for instance by exploring the FOAF ontology to obtain missing information, such as the person's gender or the project's initial date. Exploring the Semantic Web to get more and more relevant information will be crucial in any case, as a system needs to access enough information about projects (dates, duration, organization involved, type of business, etc.) to state something "interesting".

However, the information stored in ontologies such as FOAF will never be as rich as necessary for an automatic generator to be able to produce all the English sentences that might express it. One solution for fixing the "vagueness" of the Semantic Web would be to enrich ontologies so that they contain information as precise as what the English language can express; in practice, this would require us to add to generic properties such as *currentProject* properties such as projectType, involvementType, projectOrganizationType, durationScale, involvementType, etc. to pinpoint what exact term is relevant for the project, what exact type of function and involvement the person has in the project (author a book, build a company, merge two companies, head an organization, design a product, oversight a business deal, chair a conference, etc.).

Reciprocally, producing RDF statements by parsing even complex English sentences has been proven to be feasible.[14] It seems to me that it would be therefore more sensible to develop linguistic resources to formalize more and more detailed information from the texts that already exist on the Web, rather than to store a simplified and redundant version of the information already available in English form on the Web in ontologies, and then try afterwards to compute back its equivalent English sentences.

References

Tim Berners-Lee, James Hendler and Ora Lassila. 2001. The Semantic Web. In *Scientific American*, pp 29-37.

Annibale Elia, Simonetta Vietri, Alberto Postiglione, Mario Monteleone and Federica Marano. 2010. Data Mining Modular Software System. In: SWWS2010 - *Proceedings of the 2010 International Conference on Semantic Web & Web Services*. Las Vegas, Nevada, USA 12-15 luglio 2010 CSREA Press, pp 127-133.

FOAF Vocabulary Specification 0.98. 2010. Namespace Document 9 August 2010. Marco Polo Eds. Available at:`http://citeseerx.ist.psu.edu/viewdoc/download?doi=10.1.1.476.8247&rep=rep1&type=pdf`

RDF 1.1 Turtle – Terse RDF Triple LanguageTurtle. World Wide Web Consortium (W3C). 2014. Available at: `https://www.w3.org/TR/turtle`

Laurence Danlos. 1987. *The linguistic basis of Text Generation*. Studies in Natural Language Processing. Cambridge University Press Eds.

Maria Pia di Buono. 2017. Endpoint for Semantic Knowledge. In *Automatic Processing of Natural-Language Electronic Texts with NooJ*. Selected Papers from the 10th International NooJ Conference. (eds. Barone, Monteleone, Silberztein) CCIS Springer: Communication in Computer and Information Science #667, pp 223-233.

Héla Fehri, Kais Haddar and Abdelmajid Ben Hamadou. 2010. Automatic Recognition and Semantic Analysis of Arabic Named Entities. In *Applications of Finite-State Language Processing: Selected Papers from the NooJ 2008 International Conference* (Budapest, Hungaria) (eds. K. Judit, M. Silberztein, T. Varadi). Cambridge Scholars Publishing, Newcastle., UK, pp 101-113.

Claire Gardent and Perez-Beltrachini. 2017. A Statistical, Grammar-Based Approach to Mico-Planning. In *Computational Linguistics* 43:1. The MIT Press Eds, pp 1-30.

Kristina Kocijan and Marko Požega. 2015. Building Family Trees With NooJ. In *Formalising Natural Languages with NooJ 2014: Selected papers from the NooJ 2014 International Conference*, (eds. J. Monti, M. Silberztein, M. Monteleone, M. P. di Buono), Newcastle upon Tyne: Cambridge Scholars Publishing, pp 198-210.

Elena Lloret Pastor. 2011. *Text Summarization based on Human Language Technologies and its Application*. Tesis Doctorales. Universitad de Alicante Eds.

Max Silberztein. 2016a. *Formalizing Natural Languages: the NooJ approach*. ISTE-Wiley E

Max Silberztein. 2016b. *Joe loves Lea:* Transformational Analysis of Direct Transitive Sentences in *Automatic Processing of Natural-Language Electronic Texts with NooJ. NooJ 2015* (eds. T. Okrut, Y. Hetsevich, M. Silberztein, H. Stanislavenka). Communications in Computer and Information Science, vol 607. Springer, Cham, pp 55-65.

[14] NooJ has been used since 2002 to parse texts in a dozen languages and produce Semantic annotations in XML or Prolog notation, cf. for instance Fehri et al. (2010), Elia et al. (2010), Kocijan and Požega (2015), di Buono (2017).

Lexicon for Natural Language Generation in Spanish Adapted to Alternative and Augmentative Communication

Silvia García-Méndez, Milagros Fernández-Gavilanes, Enrique Costa-Montenegro, Jonathan Juncal-Martínez, Francisco J. González-Castaño
GTI Research Group, AtlantTIC
University of Vigo, 36310 Vigo, Spain
{sgarcia, mfgavilanes, kike, jonijm, javier}@gti.uvigo.es

Abstract

In this paper we present *Elsa*, the first lexicon for Spanish with morphological, syntactic and semantic information automatically generated from a well-known pictogram resource and especially tailored for Augmentative and Alternative Communication (AAC). This lexicon, focusing on that specific icon set widely used within AAC applications, is motivated by the need to improve Natural Language Generation (NLG) systems to aid people who have been diagnosed to suffer from communication disorders. In addition, we design an automatic lexicon extension procedure by means of a training process to complete the linguistic data. For this we used a dataset composed of novels and tales in Spanish, with pictogram representations, since the lexicon is meant for AAC applications for children with disabilities. Moreover, we provide the algorithms used to build our lexicon and a use case of *Elsa* within an NLG system to observe the usability of our proposal.

1 Introduction

According to the *State Database of Persons with Disabilities 2014* report[1], 14,456 Spanish people had expression problems, 72,088 had mixed disabilities and 45,818 had communication disorders (Doval, 2013). Relying on unofficial sources[2], in Spain and Mexico over 1% of children are autistic (over 800,000 people) requiring language aids. Many of these have evolved from graphical systems and rely on speech synthesis and speech recognition (Heimann Mühlenbock & Lundälv, 2011). They are known as Augmentative and Alternative Communication or AAC.

Our goal is to automatically create a Spanish vocabulary to be used in a Natural Language Generation (NLG) system applied to an AAC communicator, by merging different linguistic resources. Pictograms (used as input) act as a bridge between the lexicon and the NLG system, and help target users express themselves easily and quickly. Some previous AAC tools such as *Talk Together* or *LetMe Talk*[3] include small vocabulary packages with hand-coded knowledge, but none of them considers morphological, syntactic and semantic information when generating messages in Spanish. There is some work on language resource merging in the literature on manual and automatic management (Hughes, Souter, & Atwell, 1995; Crouch & King, 2005; Molinero, Sagot & Nicolas, 2009) but Spanish resources considering morphological, syntactic and semantic data has not been considered so far. Moreover, combining existing resources seemed a promising approach towards our goal, due to the grammatical difficulties of Spanish[4], as there are fewer resources than in English (Janssen, 2005).

The rest of this work is organised as follows. In Section 2 we review the existing linguistic resources for Spanish and the process conducted to build *Elsa*. In Section 3 we present an automatic lexicon extension procedure. Then, in Section 4 we conduct an

[1] Press release available Oct. 2016 at http://www.dependencia.imserso.es/InterPresent2/groups/imserso/documents/binario/bdepcd_2014.pdf.

[2] Press releases available Oct. 2016 at http://www.antena3.com/noticias/salud/espana-350000-personas-estan-diagnosticadas-autismo_2015040257ledda86584a8abb583c1ee.html and http://projectspectrum.net/2016/02/05/primer-estimado-de-prevalencia-de-autismo-en-mexico-es-de-1-en-115-individuos.

[3] Available at http://acecentre.org.uk/talk-together and http://www.utac.cat/descarregues/cace-utac.

[4] Some difficulties are those related to the inflection of verbs.

Proceedings of the Linguistic Resources for Automatic Natural Language Generation Workshop, pages 11–15, Santiago de Compostela, Spain, September 4, 2017.

evaluation of the created lexicon. In Section 5 we provide a use case of *Elsa* within an NLG system. Section 6 concludes the paper.

2 Reusing existing resources to build *Elsa*

The construction of *Elsa* begins with the selection of an available pictographic set for AAC users. After evaluating some possibilities[5] we choose the free and highly comprehensive *Arasaac*[6] set. Nonetheless, this dataset had to be preprocessed by removing the pictograms with the same meaning and word descriptions, whose redundancy is due to their different representation according to their colour. By doing so, we obtained our icon set with 9,411 pictograms, of which 6,970 have a single associated word (including proper names) and the rest are verbal phrases or compound proper names. Once this step is finished, it is necessary to add POS tags, syntactic and semantic information to each *Arasaac* word entry. For this purpose, we looked for available Spanish linguistic resources. We choose:

- *Adesse*[7] (García-Miguel, Vaamonde, & González Domínguez, 2010).
- Multilingual Central Repository[8] (MCR) (González-Agirre, Laparra, & Rigau, 2012).
- Lexicon of Spanish inflected forms[9] (LEFFE) (Molinero, Sagot, & Nicolas, 2009).

We start the process by extracting from each resource some information on the forms of the preprocessed icon set. Next, our approach follows the two well-defined steps (Crouch & King, 2005) between which we include a verification step: (1) we extract and map the form entries to a common format, adapted from Lexical Markup Framework (LMF) format (Francopoulo, et al., 2006); (2) we verify them at a lexical level in the DRAE[10]; and finally (3) we combine the entries once they have been found to be equivalent using the graph unification model (Necsulescu, Bel, Padró, Marimon & Revilla, 2011; Bel, Padró & Necsulescu, 2011). This operation is based on set unions of compatible feature values, allowing the validation of common information, the addition of differential information and the exclusion of inconsistencies.

The steps of extraction and mapping, verification and merging are explained in Algorithms 1, 2 and 3, respectively. In algorithm 4, we can observe the composition of the steps as explained in this Section.

Algorithm 1 Extraction and mapping

```
function EXTRACTION_MAPPING({LEFFE})
    for e_LEFFE ∈ {LEFFE} do
        lem_e_LEFFE = e_LEFFE.getLemma()
        cat_e_LEFFE = e_LEFFE.getCat()
        if cat_e_LEFFE=verb AND lem_e_LEFFE.isInAdesse()
        then
            e_ADESSE = searchInAdesse(lem_e_LEFFE)
            {ADESSE}.add(e_ADESSE)
        end if
        if cat.isAdj() OR cat.isAdv() OR cat.isN() OR
         cat.isV() AND lem_e_LEFFE.isInMCR() then
            e_MCR = searchInMcr(lem_e_LEFFE)
            {MCR}.add(e_MCR)
        end if
    end for
end function
```

Algorithm 2 Verification

```
function VERIFICATION({SET})
    for e_SET ∈ {SET} do
        lem_e_SET = e_SET.getLemma()
        cat_e_SET = e_SET.getCat()
        if !lem_e_SET.isInDRAE() OR !lem_e_SET.catInDRAE
(cat_e_SET)
        then
            {SET}.delete(e_SET)
        end if
    end for
end function
```

[5] Some of them were: *Pictographic Communication System* (`http://www.mayer-johnson.com/category/symbols-and-photos`) and *Pictogram* (`http://www.pictogram.se`), which are not free; or *Widgit* (`https://widgit.com`) with no support for Spanish.

[6] Created by the CATEDU, the *Alborada Special Education Public School* and Sergio Palao in 2008 under Creative Commons license. It contains over 16,000 pictograms with their associated words or sequence of words for Spanish, as well as multiple other languages. Available at `http://www.catedu.es/arasaac`.

[7] Database of over 3,400 verbs, diathesis alternations and syntactic semantic schemes in Spanish. Accessible at `http://adesse.uvigo.es`, May 2017.

[8] Lexical database integrating the Spanish WordNet into the EuroWordNet framework. Available at `http://adimen.si.ehu.es/web/MCR`, May 2017.

[9] A wide-coverage morphological and syntactic lexicon. Available at `https://gforge.inria.fr/frs/?group%20id=482&release%20id=4290`, May 2017.

[10] *Diccionario de la Real Academia de la Lengua Española* available at `http://www.rae.es`.

Algorithm 3 Merging

function MERGING
  $\{\text{ELSA}\} = \{\text{LEFFE}\} \cup \cup \{\text{ADESSE}\} \cup \{\text{MCR}\}$
end function

Algorithm 4 Building procedure

$\{\text{ADESSE}\} = \{\emptyset\}$, $\{\text{MCR}\} = \{\emptyset\}$
$\{\text{LEFFE}\}=$ LoadLeffe()
EXTRACTION_MAPPING({LEFFE})
$\{\text{SETS}\} = \{\{\text{LEFFE}\},\{\text{ADESSE}\},\{\text{MCR}\}\}$
for $\{\text{set}\} \in \{\text{SETS}\}$ **do**
  VERIFICATION({set})
end for
MERGING

3 Automatic lexicon extension

Keeping in mind that we intend to use this lexicon within an NLG system adapted to AAC users, and in order to facilitate the task of avoiding pictograms related to prepositions, we need to infer *a priori* which specific preposition follows a verb. The training process was performed using a dataset composed of novels and nearly five hundred tales in Spanish (Andersen, 2016; Anonymous, 2016; Grimm, 2016), previously POS-tagged applied with Freeling Tagger[11], since we plan to use the lexicon in AAC applications for children with disabilities and these are the only contents with pictogram representation. In this regard, we are able to include more options beyond those present in the subcategorization frames for verbs taken from LEFFE and *Adesse*, such as those related to figurative language approaches[12]. Since this grammar realization is not present in the selected lexica, we developed a language model from a training process, considering bigrams and trigrams around verbs and using syntactic and semantic knowledge.

4 Experimental results

In order to evaluate the quality of *Elsa*, we first measured the coverage achieved after adding the information extracted from all resources. Table 1 shows the number of lemmas that were included in each resource. Table 2 shows the coverage of *Elsa* over the icon set. Our lexicon covered almost the entire icon set and most word entries include syntactic and semantic data essential to conduct the NLG process correctly. Moreover, Table 3 shows the number of lemmas and forms classified by categories. Most lemmas (3,165) are tagged as nouns, representing 7,035 inflected forms added to *Elsa*, whereas most forms (45,341) are tagged as verbs, representing 811 lemmas.

```
<Entry lemma="desagradar">
 <fileName>desagradar.png</fileName>
 <feat att="POS" val="v"/>
 <SemSynset>
  <feat att="id" val="ili3001776727"/>
  <feat att="genSem" val="emotion"/>
  <feat att="concretSem"
   val="IntentionalPsychologicalProcess"/>
 </SemSynset>
 <WordForm>
  <feat att="writtenForm" val="desagradar"/>
  <feat att="pronominal" val="true"/>
  <feat att="transitive" val="false"/>
  <feat att="gerund" val="desagradando"/>
  <feat att="p_ms" val="desagradado"/>
  <feat att="p_mp" val="desagradados"/>
  <feat att="p_fs" val="desagradada"/>
  <feat att="p_fp" val="desagradadas"/>
  <feat att="IP1s" val="desagrado"/>
  ...
 </WordForm>
 <SCF>
  <feat att="type" val="active"/>
  <feat att="subj" val="est"/>
  <feat att="oind" val="exp"/>
 </SCF>
 <SCF_training>
  <feat att="type" val="active"/>
  <feat att="subj" val="est"/>
  <feat att="a_oind" val="exp"/>
 </SCF_training>
</Entry>
```

Figure 1: Fragment of the entry for the Spanish lemma *desagradar* 'displease' in *Elsa*

Figure 1 shows an example in adapted LMF format of the word entry *desagradar* 'displease' with morphological, syntactic and semantic data. *SemSynset* contains the semantic information from MCR. In addition to the conjugation in *WordForm*, *SCF* contains the syntactic information on the verb after combining the data extracted from LEFFE and *Adesse*. There is only one possible realization in the active form, where the subject is an *estímulo* 'stim-

[11] A library that provides multiple language analysis services, including probabilistic prediction of categories in unknown words (Atserias et al., 2006; Padró & Stanilovsky, 2012).

[12] For example the verb *comer* 'eat' whose subcategorization frames did not include the possibility of using the preposition *a* with people, even though it is widely employed in tales, as in the clause *El lobo se comío a la abuelita* 'The wolf ate the granny'.

Category	LEFFE		Adesse		MCR	
	Number	%	Number	%	Number	%
Adjective	824	98.92%	-	-	503	60.38%
Adverb	59	100.00%	-	-	46	77.97%
Noun	3,129	98.86%	-	-	2,957	93.43%
Verb	809	99.75%	731	90.14%	791	97.53%

Table 1: Lemmas of *Elsa* included in the different resources by lexical category

ulus' and the verb is followed by an indirect object[13] that is an *experimentador* 'experimenter'.

In *SCF_training*, a new preposition, *a* 'to' (not present in any of the selected resources), was inferred in order to use it within the subcategorization frame of the verb (before the indirect object `oind`). In addition, the *Elsa* entry *desagradar* 'displease' is linked to a pictogram image file from the icon set.

Included	Single word	Compound
in *Elsa*	4,434	684
not in *Elsa*	1,716	1,167
TOTAL	**6,150**	**1,851**

Table 2: *Elsa* coverage of the AAC icon set

	Category	Lemmas	Forms
Elsa	Adjective	833	2,583
	Adverb	59	59
	Conjunction	15	15
	Determiner	23	71
	Noun	3,165	7,035
	Preposition	20	20
	Pronoun	16	47
	Proper name	171	171
	Verb	811	45,341
	TOTAL	**5,298**	**55,342**

Table 3: *Elsa* size by category

5 *Elsa* use case: NLG system

Assuming that our system input is: *tiempo, desagradar, profesor, ayer* 'weather, displease, teacher, yesterday'.

- System output **using *Elsa***: *El tiempo desagradó al profesor ayer* 'The weather displeased the teacher yesterday'.
- System output without **using *Elsa***: *El tiempo desagradar el profesor ayer* 'The weather displease the teacher yesterday' (where displease is the infinitive of the verb).

In this example, the system can determine that *desagradar* 'displease' is a verb, whose subject is *tiempo* 'weather', followed by an indirect object *profesor* 'teacher'. In addition, this verb needs the preposition *a* 'to' because *profesor* 'teacher' is a person. Besides, the presence of the adverb *ayer* 'yesterday' indicates that the tense is past. Our system would neither infer the additional elements needed nor the correct morphological inflections related to the syntactic and semantic features without the linguistic information provided by *Elsa*.

6 Conclusions

Elsa is an approach for lexica generation specially tailored for the needs of AAC applications. Besides including several types of linguistic information (morphology, syntax and semantics), a training process was executed to complete the subcategorization frames for verbs, like those present in figurative language. The resulting lexicon may be useful for assisting people with communication disabilities through NLG systems. In order to increase efficiency and precision, additional linguistic resources can be easily integrated due to the fact that the building process is automatic. To complete the semantic information, we propose to establish synonymy relations between the word entries to reuse their semantic classification and fill in the missing information.

[13] In Spanish an intransitive verb has not direct object but it may be followed by an indirect object or other complements.

Acknowledgments

This work was partially supported by a grant from Ministerio de Economía, Industria y Competitividad, Spain (TEC2016-76465-C2-2-R); and by Xunta de Galicia grant (GRC2014/046).

References

Andersen. 2016. *Fairy tales of Hans Christian Andersen* (Spanish). Available 28/11/2016 at `https://es.wikisource.org/wiki/Cuentos_clásicos_para_niños`.

Anonymous. 2016. *Traditional Spanish tales.* Available 28/11/2016 at `http://loscuentostradicionales.blogspot.com.es`.

Jordi Atserias, Bernardino Casas, Elisabet Comelles, Meritxell González, Lluís Padró, and Muntsa Padró. 2006. Freeling 1.3: Syntactic and semantic services in an open-source NLP library. In *Proceedings of the fifth international conference on Language Resources and Evaluation* (LREC 2006), Genoa, Italy, ELRA, pp 48-55.

Nuria Bel, Muntsa Padró, and Silvia Necsulescu. 2011. A method towards the fully automatic merging of lexical resources. In *Proceedings of Workshop on Language Resources, Technology and Services in the Sharing Paradigm.* ACL, Chiang Mai, Thailand, pp 8-15.

Dick Crouch and Tracy Holloway King. 2005. Unifying lexical resources. In *Proceedings of Interdisciplinary Workshop on the Identification and Representation of Verb Features and Verb Classes.* Saarbrücken, Germany, pp 32-37.

Gil Francopoulo, Nuria Bel, Monte George, Nicoletta Calzolari, Monica Monachini, Mandy Pet, and Claudia Soria. 2006. Lexical markup framework (LMF) for NLP multilingual resources. In *Proceedings of the Workshop on Multilingual Language Resources and Interoperability*, MLRI '06, Stroudsburg, PA, USA. Association for Computational Linguistics, pp 1-8.

Fátima María García Doval. 2013. *Aportaciones didácticas de un tablero digital para personas con dificultades de competencia comunicativa.* Ph.D. thesis, University of Santiago de Compostela.

José M. García-Miguel, Gael Vaamonde, and Fita González Domínguez. 2010. Adesse, a database with syntactic and semantic annotation of a corpus of Spanish. In *Proceedings of the 7th International Conference on Language Resources and Evaluation* (LREC'10) (eds. N. Calzolari, K. Choukri, B. Maegaard, J. Mariani, J. Odijk, S. Piperidis, M. Rosner, and D. Tapias), Valletta, Malta. European Language Resources Association (ELRA), pp 1903-1910.

Aitor González-Agirre, Egoitz Laparra, and German Rigau. 2012. Multilingual central repository version 3.0: upgrading a very large lexical knowledge base. In *6th Global WordNet Conference*, Matsue, Japan, pp 118-125.

Grimm. 2016. *Grimm's fairy tales* (Spanish). Available 28/11/2016 at `http://www.grimmstories.com/es`.

Katarina Heimann Mühlenbock and Mats Lundälv. 2011. *Using lexical and corpus resources for augmenting the AAC lexicon.* In Proceedings of the Second Workshop on Speech and Language Processing for Assistive Technologies, SLPAT '11, Edinburgh, Scotland, UK. Association for Computational Linguistics, pp 120-127.

John Hughes, Clive Souter, and Eric Atwell. 1995. Automatic extraction of tagset mappings from parallel annotated corpora. In *From Texts to Tags: Issues in Multilingual Language Analysis. Proceedings of SIGDAT Workshop in Conjunction with the 7h Conference of the European Chapter of the Association for Computational Linguistics.* University College Dublin, Ireland, pp 10-17.

Maarten Janssen. 2005. Open source lexical information network. In *Proceedings of the 3rd International Workshop on Generative Approaches to the Lexicon*, Geneva, Switzerland, pp 400-410. `http://ww.cibercursoslp.com/Papers/GL2005-mjanssen.pdf`. Date Accessed: April 18, 2017.

Miguel A. Molinero, Benoît Sagot, and Lionel Nicolas. 2009. A morphological and syntactic wide-coverage lexicon for Spanish: The Leffe. In *RANLP 2009 - Recent Advances in Natural Language Processing*, Borovets, Bulgaria, September, pp 264-269.

Silvia Necsulescu, Nuria Bel, Muntsa Padró, Montserra Marimon, and Eva Revilla. 2011. Towards the automatic merging of language resources. In *Proceedings of 1st International Workshop on Lexical Resources: an ESSLLI 2011 Workshop*, Ljubljana, Slovenia, pp 7-77.

Lluís Padró and Evgeny Stanilovsky. 2012. Freeling 3.0: Towards wider multilinguality. In *Proceedings of the Language Resources and Evaluation Conference* (LREC 2012), Istanbul, Turkey. ELRA, pp 2473-2479.

Generating Answering Patterns from Factoid Arabic Questions

Essia Bessaies, Slim Mesfar, Henda Ben Ghezala*
Riadi Laboratory, *ENSI,
University of Manouba Tunisia
{essia.bessaies, slim.mesfar}@riadi.rnu.tn;
*henda.benghezala@ensi.rnu.tn

Abstract

This works deals with Arabic factoid Question Answering systems (QA). Commonly, the task of QA is divided into three phases: question analysis, answer pattern generation, and answer extraction. Each phase plays a crucial role in overall performance. In this paper, we focus on the two first phases: Question Analysis and Answer Pattern Generation. We used the NooJ platform which represents a valuable linguistic development environment. The first evaluations show that the actual results are encouraging and could be deployed for more types of questions other than factoid ones.

1 Introduction

In recent years, the medical domain has a high volume of electronic documents. Managing this large quantity of data makes the search of specific information complex and time consuming. This complexity is especially evident when we seek a short and precise answer to a human natural language question rather than a full list of documents and web pages. In this case, the user requirement could be a Question Answering (QA) system which represents a specialized area in the field of information retrieval.

The goal of a QA system is to provide inexperienced users with a flexible access to information allowing them to write a query in natural language and obtain not the documents which contain the answer, but its precise answer passage from input texts. There has been a lot of research in English as well as some European language QA systems. However, Arabic QA systems (Brini et al., 2009) could not match the pace due to some inherent difficulties with the language itself as well as due to lack of tools available to assist researchers. Therefore, the current project attempts to design and develop the modules of an Arabic QA system.

In this paper, we present a linguistic approach for analyzing medical questions and generating answer patterns from factoid Arabic questions.

In the first section, we give a short insight about Arabic NLP specificities followed by an overview of state-of-the-art developments. In section 3, we describe the generic architecture of the proposed QA system. Section 4 introduces our approach to the annotation of medical factoid questions and the generation of answering patterns.

In this section, we describe how we analyze a given question by means of the application of a cascade of morpho-syntactic grammars. The linguistic patterns depicted in these grammars allow us to annotate the question in order to extract its type (time, quantity …), its topic, as well as its focus. After examining the generation of response patterns from these extracted key words (Type, Topic and Focus), the results of our experiments are described in section 5.

2 Current Research

As explained in the introduction, QA systems present a good solution for textual information retrieval, knowledge sharing, and discovery. Current research deals with two challenging topics: the Arabic natural language processing in the medical domain and the second concerns QA systems.

2.1 The Arabic language

The Arabic language is a member of the Semitic language family and it is the most widely spoken one with almost 300 million first language speakers. The Arabic language has its own script (written from right to left) using a 28 letters alphabet (25 consonants and 3 long vowels) with allographic variants and diacritics which are used as short vowels

Proceedings of the Linguistic Resources for Automatic Natural Language Generation Workshop, pages 17–24, Santiago de Compostela, Spain, September 4, 2017.

except one diacritic which is used as a double consonant marker. The Arabic script does not support capitalization that could help researchers identify named entities, for example. Numbers, however, are written from left to right which presents a real challenge for Arabic text editors to handle words written from right to left and numbers from left to right.

2.2 Arabic QA systems

QA systems for Arabic are very few. Mainly, it is due to the lack of accessibility to linguistic resources, such as freely available lexical resources, corpora and basic NLP tools (tokenizers, morphological analyzers, etc.).

To our knowledge, there are only five research works on Arabic QA systems.

- QARAB (Hammo et al., 2002) is an Arabic QA system that that takes factoid Arabic questions and attempts to provide short answers. QARAB uses both information retrieval and natural language processing techniques.

- ArabiQA (Benajiba et al., 2007), which is fully oriented to the modern Arabic language, also answers factoid questions using Named Entity Recognition. However, this system is not yet completed.

- DefArabicQA (Trigui et al., 2010) provides short answers to Arabic natural language questions. This system provides effective and exact answers to definition questions expressed in Arabic from Web resources. DefArabicQA identifies candidate definitions by using a set of lexical patterns, filters these candidate definitions by using heuristic rules and ranks them by using a statistical approach. It only processes definition questions and does not include other types of question (When, How and Why).

- AQuASys (Bekhti and Alharbi, 2013) is composed of three modules: A question analysis module, a sentence filtering module and an answer extraction module. Special consideration has been given to improving the accuracy of the question analysis and the answer extraction scoring phases. These phases are crucial in terms of finding the correct answer. The recall rate is 97.5% and the precision rate is 66.25%.

- Yes/No Arabic Question Answering System (Kurdi, et al, 2014) is a formal model for a semantic based yes/no Arabic question answering system based on paragraph retrieval. The results are based on 20 documents. It shows a positive result of about 85% when we use entire documents. Besides, it gives 88% when we use only paragraphs. The system focuses only on yes/no questions and the corpus size is relatively small (20 documents).

After this investigation into QA systems, we aim to develop a QA system based on a linguistic approach. It uses NooJ's linguistic engine in order to formalize the automatic recognition rules for question analysis. The named entity recognizer (NER) is embedded in our QA system in order to annotate the factoid questions and associate them with the extracted named entities. For this purpose, we have adapted a rules based approach to recognize Arabic named entities. Furthermore, we aim to generate the potential answer patterns using the paraphrasing and transformation module in the NooJ platform (Silberztein, 2015).

3 Proposed Architecture for our QA System

From a general viewpoint, the design of a QA system (Figure 1) must take into account three phases:

Question analysis: This module performs a morphological analysis to determine the question class. A question class helps the system to classify the question type to provide a suitable answer. This module may also identify additional semantic features of the question like the topic and the focus.

Answer pattern generation: After analyzing the question and extracting the key words (e.g., focus and topic) from a given factoid question, the system generates response patterns from these extracted key words. Our approach automatically generates patterns using NooJ's linguistic engine.

Answer extraction: This module selects the most accurate answers among the phrases in a given corpus. The selection is based on the question analysis. The suggested answers are then given to the user as a response to his initial natural language query.

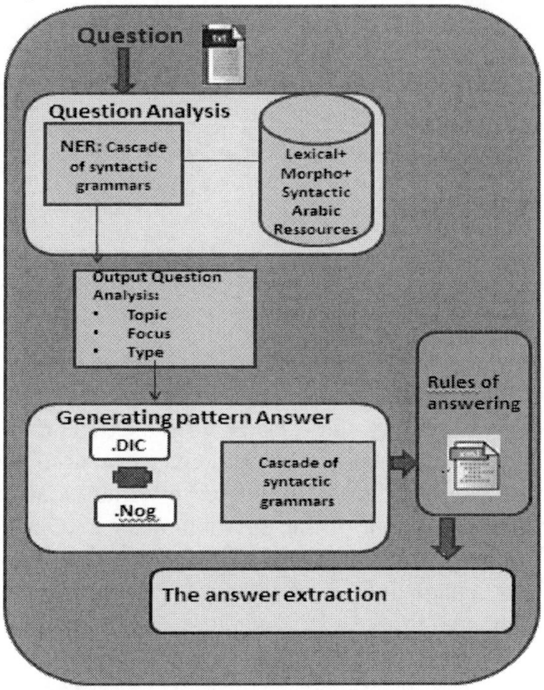

Figure 1: Architecture for our QA System

In this paper, we explore only the first two phases.

4 Preconized processing approach

4.1 Question Analysis

Our approach uses the NooJ development platform. It allows us to build various required resources (dictionaries, morpho-syntactic grammars, etc.) and perform a linguistic analysis on a given corpus.

In addition to the linguistic resources in NooJ's Arabic module (Mesfar, 2010), we added specific properties in lexical entries for the needs of the current project. For instance, some additional information must be added to entries:

1. Nominal predicate information
   - **Npred** = Nominal predicate information
2. Synonyms
   - **Syn**=Synonyms of focus
3. Support verbs (that will be used to generate paraphrases)
   - **Sup**=Support verbs

Example

- إِكْتَشَفَ, V+FLX+NPred=اِكْتَشَاف +Syn1= أَوْجَدَ +Sup1=وَقَعَ +Sup2=تَمَّ +sup3=قَامَ بِـ

These enhanced lexical resources are used next within a cascade of morpho-syntactic grammars.

Named Entity Recognition:

We think that an integration of a Named Entity Recognition (NER) module will definitely boost system performance. It is also very important to point out that an NER is required as a tool for almost all the QA system components. Those NER systems allow extracting proper nouns as well as temporal and numeric expressions from raw text (Mesfar, 2007). In our case, we used our own NER system especially formulated for the Arabic medical domain. We have considered six proper names categories: organization, location, person, viruses, diseases, and treatment (Table 1).

Categories	Definitions	Examples
Organization	Names of corporattions, gov. entities or ONGs	بنك ألدم = blood bank
Location	Politically or geographically defined locations	مستشفى الأطفال = Children's Hospital
Person	Names of persons or families	طبيب النساء علي طارق = Gynecologist Tariq Ali
Viruses	Names of medical viruses	فيروس الروتا = Rotavirus
Diseases	Names of diseases, illness, sickness	مرض السرطان = Cancer
Treatment	Names of medical viruses	علاج طبيعى = Physiotherapist

Table 1: Named Entity Recognition

Automatic annotation of question using NooJ's syntactic grammars

Our approach focuses on the problem of finding document snippets that answer a particular category of fact-seeking questions or factoid questions, for example simple interrogative questions with a named entity (Timex, Numex or Enamex). The choice of factoid questions versus other types of questions is motivated by the following factors:

- A considerable percentage of the questions actually submitted to a search engine are factoid questions. Current search engines are only able to return links to full-length documents rather than brief document fragments that answer the user's question.

- The frequent occurrence of factoid questions in daily usage is confirmed by the composition of the question test sets in the QA track at TREC[1]. The percentage of questions that are factoid questions grew in TREC.

- Most recent approaches to open-domain QA use NER as a foundation for detecting candidate answers.

As far as current research is concerned, our QA module accepts, as input, only Arabic factoid questions. Then, in order to look for the best answer, it gives the maximum amount of information (syntactic, semantic, distributional, etc.) from the given question, such as the expected answer type, and the focus and topic of the question. This information will play an important role in the generation of potential answer patterns.

- **Type:** the type corresponds to the type of question (time, person, organization, etc.)

- **Topic:** the topic corresponds to the subject matter of the question.

- **Focus**: the focus corresponds to the specific property of the topic that the user is looking for.

The following example shows the detailed annotation of the identified parts of a question.

Example

- When was cancer discovered?

متى اكتشف مرض السرطان؟

متى (when): Factoid+Time <ENAMEX+MEDIC> <V> <ADV+TIME>

اكتشف (Was discovered) : Focus

مرض السرطان (The cancer disease) : Topic

4.2 Generating answer patterns

Arabic sentences are usually complex and very long. This sets up obstacles for the extraction of a short and precise answer for a given question. Thus, we chose to generate answer patterns associated with the output of our question analysis. Our preliminary observations on sentence structure showed that a huge number of response structures could be extracted from Arabic texts.

These structures depend on author origins (native language, geographical zone of Arabic studies, etc). Hence, generating answer patterns could be an interesting alternative to identify the different structures and answer patterns (see Table 2).

The example provided in Table 2 consolidates the main objective of this project which consists in developing a context-sensitive and linguistically enhanced paraphrase generator. First, this generator uses the annotated sequences within the question analysis phase (recognized syntactic-semantic sequences, named entities, multi-words and other phrasal units). Then, it transforms them into semantically equivalent phrases, expressions, or sentences. This output produces potential answer patterns based on the original question's topic and focus.

For instance, these generated patterns will use the predicate noun, synonyms as well as the related support verbs shown in the annotation of focus or topic.

[1] Text Retrieval Conference is an ongoing series of workshops focusing on different types of information retrieval (IR), research areas, or tracks.

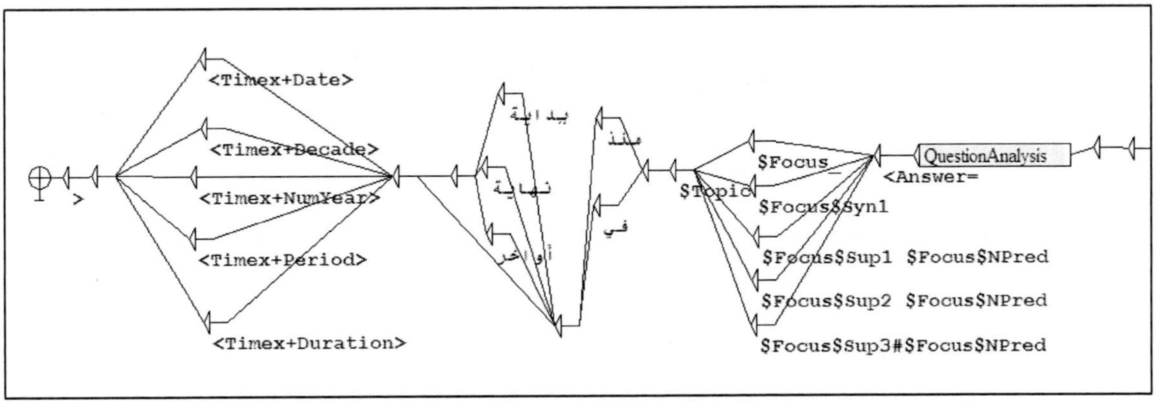

Figure 2: Sub-graph of answer pattern generation (syntactic grammar)

Question:	
متى وقع إكتشاف مرض السيدا ؟	When did the discovery of AIDS occur?

Some answer structures:	
وقع إكتشاف مرض السيدا في سنة 1981	The discovery of Aids occurred in 1981.
إكتشف مرض السيدا في سنة 1981	The discovery of Aids was in year 1981.
تم إكتشاف مرض السيدَا في سنة 1981	The discovery of aids was made in 1981
إكتشف مرض الإيداز منذ بداية الثمانينات	AIDS has been discovered since the early 80's
منذ سنة 1981 إكتشف مرض الإيداز	Since 1981, he has discovered AIDS
في بداية الثمانينات وقع إكتشاف مرض السيدا	In the early 80's the discovery of SIDA occurred
وقع إكتشاف مرض السيدا في الثمانينات	The discovery of SIDA occurred in the 1980s
تم إكتشاف مرض السيدا في الثمانينات	SIDA was discovered in the 80's
في سنة 1981إكتشف مرض السيدا	In 1981 he discovered Aids.
مرض السيدا يعتبر من الأمراض التي إكتشافها في بداية الثمانينات	Aids is one of the diseases that were discovered in the early 1980s.

Table 2: Example of generated example patterns

If we consider the previous example (Table 2), we can take advantage of the focus's annotation information (إكْتَشَفَ – to discover) to generate:

- إكْتَشَاف **(discovery)** : the nominal predicate
- أَوْجَدَ **(to find)** : a synonym
- وَقَعَ **(to occur)** : a support verb that can be used in conjunction with the predicate noun (discovery)

Based on the information associated with the different parts of the question, we generate answer patterns with respect to the potential phrase structures (nominal, verbal, prepositional, adverbial, active or passive phrases). In fact, this task takes into consideration the type of answer expected by the user, and this means that the answer extraction module will perform differently for each type of question.

The sub-graph illustrated in Figure 2 with NooJ's graphical editor, shows that the sub-graph called "Question Analysis" that stores the question parts in two variables: $Topic (contains the topic of our question) and $Focus (contains the special focus of the current question). Then, we proceed to the pattern generation where we use the related information (syntactic, semantic, distributional as well as synonymy and/or lexicon-grammar properties). In order to display the needed information, we build a combination of output patterns using the following variables:

- $Focus$Syn1
- $Focus$NPred
- $Focus$Sup

Finally, we add the potential combination of response parts (in the given example, we added Timex expressions)

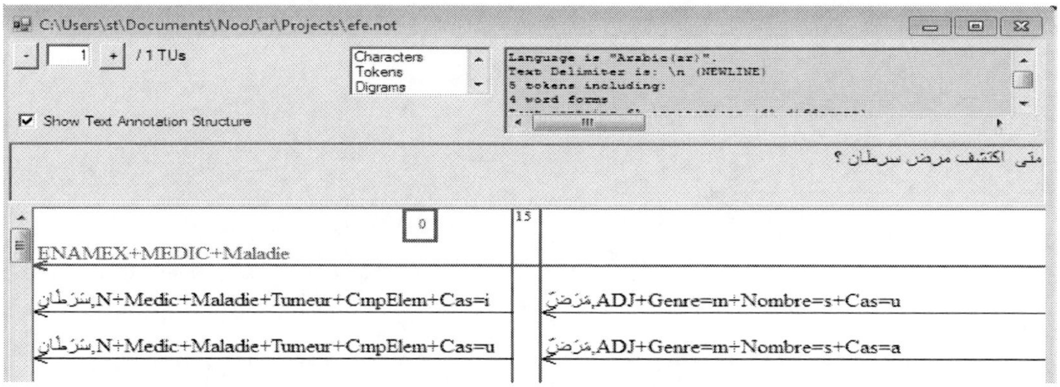

Figure 3: Text Annotation Structure

5 Experiments and Results

5.1 Question analysis

Named Entity Recognition (NER)

The ENAMEX+MEDIC grammar is launched automatically during the linguistic analysis, in order to annotate the sequences and expressions recognized by the transducers corresponding to the grammar launched (Figure 3).

To evaluate our NER local grammars, we analyzed our corpus to extract manually all named entities. Then, we compare the results of our system with those obtained by manual extraction. The application of our cascade of local grammars gives the results as shown in Table 3.

Precision	Recall	F-Measure
0.90	0.82	0.88

Table 3: NER grammar experiments

According to these results (Table 3), we obtain acceptable scores for named entities recognition. Our evaluation shows an F-measure of 0.88. This result is encouraging given the rate achieved by the systems participating in MUC[2].

Discussion

- Despite the problems described above, the techniques used seem to be adequate and display very encouraging recognition rates. Indeed, a minority of the rules may be sufficient to cover a large part of the patterns and ensure coverage. However, many other rules must be added to improve recall.

Automatic annotation of factoid question in standard Arabic

To evaluate our automatic annotation of questions using local grammars, we compare the results of our system with those obtained by manual extraction (Figure 4).

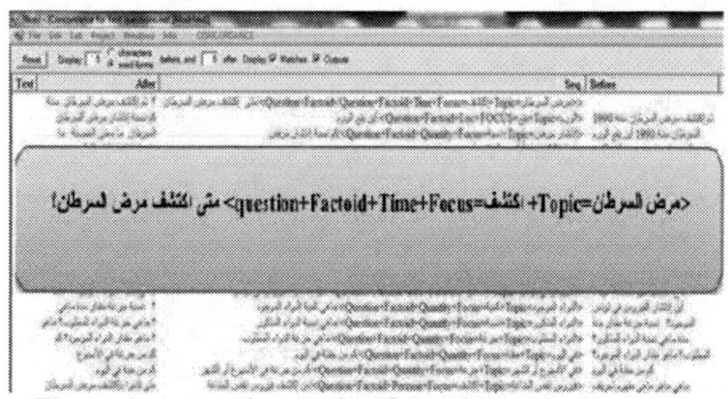

Figure 4: Annotation results of question analysis syntactic grammar (NooJ Grammar).

The application of our local grammar gives the result as shown in Table 4.

Precision	Recall	F-Measure
0.75	0.72	0.73

Table 4: Annotation of factoid question experiments

According to these results (Table 4), we obtain an acceptable annotation rate for the cascade of morpho-syntactic grammars. Our evaluation shows an F-measure of 0.73. We note that the rate of silence in the corpus is low, which is represented by the recall value 0.72.

[2] The Message Understanding Conferences.

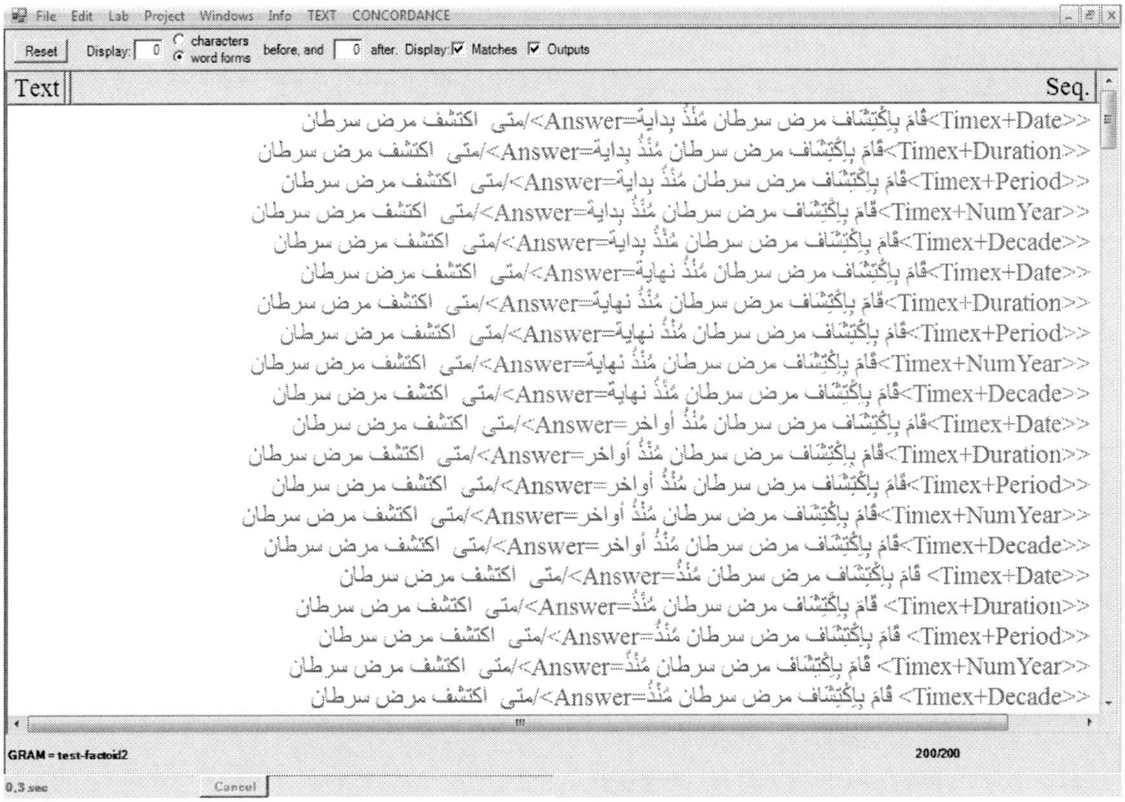

Figure 5: Result of Generating answer patterns

This is due to the fact that this assessment is mainly based on the results of the NER module.

Discussion

Errors are often due to the complexity of user's questions or the absence of their structure in our system In fact, Arabic sentences are usually very long, which sets up obstacles for question analysis. Despite the problems described above, the developed method seems to be adequate and shows very encouraging extraction rates. However, other rules must be added to improve the result.

5.2 Generating answer patterns

For the already described example, we generate hundreds of answer pattern combinations (Figure 5). At this stage of our research, we can't deny that some further patterns are not yet covered by our grammar. This is due to the fact that this assessment is mainly based on the results of the question analysis module and the NER module.

Despite the problems described above, the developed system seems to be adequate and shows very encouraging extraction rates. However, other rules and other keywords (synonyms, supports verbs, etc.) have to be improved in our next steps.

6 Conclusion

Arabic QA systems could not match the pace due to some inherent difficulties with the language itself, as well as the lack of tools offered to support researchers. The task of our QA system can be divided into three phases: question analysis, answer pattern generation, and answer extraction. Each of these phases plays crucial roles in overall performance of the QA system. In this paper, we focused on the first two phases: question analysis and answer pattern generation.

In the near future, we aim to apply the generated patterns to a real corpus in order to deal with the answer extraction phase. We will consider such methods used in answer extraction including tools, evaluation, and corpus.

This will show the viability of the current research results and give real answers to end users. Finally, as a long term ambition, we intend to consider processing "why" and "how" question types.

References

Sman Bekhti and Maryam Alharbi. 2013. Aquasys: A question answering system for Arabic. In Proceedings of WSeas International Conference. *Recent Advances in Computer Engineering Series*, no. 12. WSEAS, pp 130-139

Yassine Benajiba, Paolo Rosso and Abdelouahid Lyhyaoui. 2007. Implementation of the ArabiQA Question Answering System's components. In *Proceedings of the Workshop on Arabic Natural Language Processing, 2nd Information Communication Technologies Int. Symposium*, ICTIS-2007, Fez, Morroco, pp 3-5.

Wissal Brini, Mariem Ellouze, Slim Mesfar and Lamia Belguith. 2009. An Arabic question-answering system for factoid questions. In *Natural Language Processing and Knowledge Engineering*, 2009. NLP-KE 2009. International Conference on. IEEE, 2009, pp 1-7.

Bassam Hammou, Hani Abu-Salem and Steven Lytinen. 2002. QARAB: A Question answering system to support the ARABic language. In *Proceedings of the workshop on Computational approaches to Semitic languages*, ACL, Philadelphia, pp 55-65.

Heba Kurdi, Sara Alkhaider and Nada Alfaifi. 2014. Development and evaluation of a web based question answering system for Arabic language. In *Computer Science & Information Technology* (CS & IT), vol. 4, no. 2, pp 187-202.

Slim Mesfar. 2007. Named Entity Recognition for Arabic Using Syntactic Grammars. *NLDB 2007*, pp 305-316.

Slim Mesfar. 2010. Towards a Cascade of Morpho-syntactic Tools for Arabic Natural Language Processing. *CICLing* 2010, pp 150-162

Max Silberztein. 2015. *La formalisation des langues : l'approche de NooJ*. Londres: ISTE.

Omar Trigui, Lamia Hadrich Belguith and Paolo Rosso. 2010. DefArabicQA: Arabic Definition Question Answering System. In *Proceedings of the Workshop on Language Resources and Human Language Technologies for Semitic Languages*, 7th LREC, Valletta, Malta, pp 40-45.

Language Generation from DB Query

Kristina Kocijan*, Božo Bekavac, Krešimir Šojat
*Department of Information and Communication Sciences
Department of Linguistics
Faculty of Humanities and Social Sciences, University of Zagreb
{krkocijan, bbekavac, ksojat}@ffzg.hr

Abstract

This paper demonstrates how to generate natural language sentences from the pieces of data found in databases in the domain of flight tickets. By using NooJ to add context to specific customer data found in customer data sets, we are able to produce sentences that give a short textual summary of each customer, providing a list of possible suggestions how to proceed. In addition, due to the rich morphology of Croatian, we are giving special attention to matching gender, number and case information where appropriate. Thus, we are able to provide individualized and grammatically correct text in spite of the customer gender or the number of tickets bought and inquiries made. We believe that such short NL overviews can help ticket sellers get a quicker assessment of the type of a customer and allow for the exchange of information with more confidence and greater speed.

1 Introduction

Ever since we have started using computers for language processing, language generation, even in its most primitive form as canned text (Jurafsky and Martin, 2000), was an exciting thing to do. Since its early beginnings in the 1950's, we have made big steps trying to make language generation more adaptable to context i.e. to build systems that can produce a set of appropriate forms and choose the right context-dependent one (Jurafsky and Martin, 2000; Bateman and Zock, 2003; Perera and Nand, 2017; Gatt and Krahmer, 2017). In this paper we will present one such project that maps non-linguistic source into the linguistic form as described in Bateman and Zock (2003).

For this purpose we are using NooJ, a linguistic development environment software. NooJ is not new to language generation (Silberztein, 2012). Due to the power of a transducer that it uses, in collaboration with variables, it has been used in different transformational projects in a variety of languages; from paraphrasing for Portuguese-English machine translation projects (Barreiro, 2008), generating transformations from Italian frozen sentences (Vietri, 2012), or paraphrasing standard Arabic in biomedical texts (Boujelben et al., 2012) to transformation of English direct transitive sentences (Silberztein, 2016a).

This paper focuses on the generation of natural language sentences from databases with records on booking and buying flight tickets. The natural language that we deal with is Croatian, a South Slavic language with rich inflectional and derivational morphology and relatively free word order. Although Croatian is basically a SOV language, word order in sentences can vary due to extensive morphosyntactic marking of major parts of speech and rules of agreement. Agreement in gender, number and person plays an important role in the project presented here. In this paper we describe the generation of brief summaries of previous customers' inquiries and actual purchase of air flight tickets expressed in the natural language.

The paper is structured as follows: after the short introduction, in section 2 we provide the information on what is behind the scenes of the NLG system we propose. In section 3 we present some aspects concerning the usage of the system in real-life environment. In Sections 4, 5 and 6 we continue with the presentation of different parts of the system that will be accompanied with a short discussion explaining the procedures. The paper concludes with an outline of future work.

Proceedings of the Linguistic Resources for Automatic Natural Language Generation Workshop, pages 25–32, Santiago de Compostela, Spain, September 4, 2017.

2 Behind the NLG proposed system

Vayre et al. (2017) give a detailed account of procedures in the building of NLG systems and point out that it normally consist of typical stages. The procedures that are thereby applied can be divided into macro-planning and micro-planning. Macro-planning comprises content selection and document structuring, whereas micro-planning usually refers to the design of syntactic constructions, lexicalization, generation of referring expression, morphological adaptation etc. Morphological adaptation is one of the procedures applied in the design of overall surface realization. Apart from morphological modifications, this last stage also includes typographical adjustment and formatting and provides the final form of the text.

Morphological adjustment (e.g. generation of inflected forms through gender/number or verb/subject agreements) is particularly important for the NLG in our system since Croatian is a highly inflected language with numerous inflectional patterns. Paradigms for nominal parts of speech consist of 7 cases in singular and plural, whereas verbs are inflected for person, number and tense. Some verbal forms, i.e. past participles, are also inflected for gender. Morphosyntactically, NPs as subjects and verbs as predicates agree in the grammatical categories of person and number, whereas verbs determine the case of NPs as objects. NPs as subjects and verbs as predicates also agree in gender if a verbal form consists of an auxiliary verb and a past participle. We can demonstrate this with the following examples:

1. He has bought seven tickets.
   On *je kupi-**o** sedam karata.*

2. She has bought seven tickets.
   Ona *je kupi-**la** sedam karata.*

3. They have bought two tickets.
   Oni *su kupi-**li** dvije karte.*

4. They have bought two tickets.
   One *su kupi-**le** dvije karte.*

As these examples show, the endings of verbal participles are modified according to the subject's number and gender. The subjects in sentences 3 and 4 are the same in English, but they differ in Croatian (in sentence 3 the subject can refer only to masculine and masculine and female gender, whereas the subject in 4 refers solely to feminine).

Sentences 3 and 4 also demonstrate another feature that must be taken into account in the linguistic design of NLG component of our system. Synchronically, the number categories in Croatian are singular and plural. However, earlier stages of language development are manifested in noun forms for plural when quantifiers are numbers two, three and four, and all the other numbers ending in these digits (e.g. 52, 23, 134 etc.). Although these nouns are in the plural, their inflected forms are similar to genitive singular. In these cases there is an evidence of paucal number. For example:

5. He has bought **one ticket.**
   *On je kupio **jednu kartu**.*

6. He has bought **two / three / four tickets.**
   *On je kupio **dvije / tri / četiri karte.***

7. He has bought **five tickets.**
   *On je kupio **pet karata.***

These linguistic issues were taken into consideration in the morphological and syntactic component of our NLG system. A more detailed account is given in section 4.

In the building of the system described in this paper, we were also guided by four major choices that NLG systems must or should make, as defined in Jurafsky and Martin (2000) and Reiter and Dale (2000):

- Content selection – in this case, our content is already provided for the system (*the system is used by ticket sellers only, and ticket buyers have no access to it*);
- Lexical selection – system is choosing a lexical item provided in the set-up pool of items depending on the value of available fields;
- Sentence structure – system produces smaller chunks that are combined into full sentences with appropriate referring (*gender of pronoun referring*) and syntactic features (*tense, number, case*);

- Discourse structure – system combines multiple sentences providing coherent structure (*introducing conjunctions to produce smooth and continuous text*).

In order to deal with one of the main problems of NLG, i.e. control of choosing among the provided alternatives of generated text (Bateman and Zock, 2003), we have found the possibility of using the NooJ linguistic environment coupled with Angular JavaScript Framework as the workable option for our domain scenario.

3 Practical usage

Applications that incorporate NLG systems can significantly speed up the usage of data stored in various databases. The importance of attending to the presentation of such information to the end user and how it can influence the user's cognitive load is well justified by Vayre et al. (2017). As mentioned, the NLG system discussed here is used by sales agents employed by a travel agency. Number of information items and their formatting should not work against them, but rather help them do their job better, faster and with more confidence. One of the ways to help them in that endeavor is to decrease the linguistic complexity of the text that is automatically generated by the system.

The data about customers who buy air tickets either online, by telephone or e-mails, are stored in the database. Since the interpretation of unprocessed data is difficult and time-consuming, there is a significant risk of poor quality of service and a potential loss of clients. Agents dealing with a large number of customers on a daily basis need a straightforward representation of their previous activities in order to improve their productivity and to maintain high quality of service. Thus, a system capable of summarizing and presenting relevant data from databases in an easily understandable form is crucial for the overall improvement of agent-customer relationship.

During the processing of customers' requests, the system automatically recognizes and classifies clients into four categories – golden, silver, bronze and regular defined in the [*Recommendations*] subgraph (Figure 1). This categorization is based on their previous activities (booked and / or purchased tickets, intervals, years, amount of money spent etc.). On the basis of these data the system provides information as to whether a customer is entitled to air tickets at reduced prices or completely free of charge.

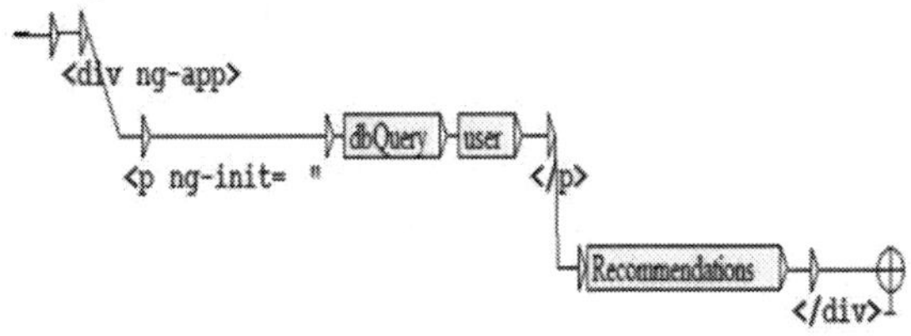

Figure 1: The main grammar

Overviews of previous activities and actual purchases, i.e. short summaries of customers' activities and status as described above, comprise four or five simple and unambiguous sentences in Croatian. These sentences contain all the data relevant for various discounted or special offers for clients, both regular and occasional. The design of the system is discussed in the next section.

4 Building the NLG section

Since we are preparing our results to be used in the network environment, we needed to incorporate all the html tags in our output as well. The main grammar (Error! Reference source not found.) consists of three main sections (subgraphs) that are connected in a manner to support the following logic:

1. recognize the query results and prepare them for initialization in the <p ng-init> tag [subgraph: *dbQuery*];

2. check the user's gender and generate the appropriate gender of a noun, verb and a pronoun in the user's description paragraph [subgraph: *user*];

3. check the user's gender and prepare the appropriate recommendations [subgraph: *Recommendations*].

Within the subgraph [*dbQuery*] (Figure 2) we are recognizing values that exist for the user and that are important to our evaluation of that user.

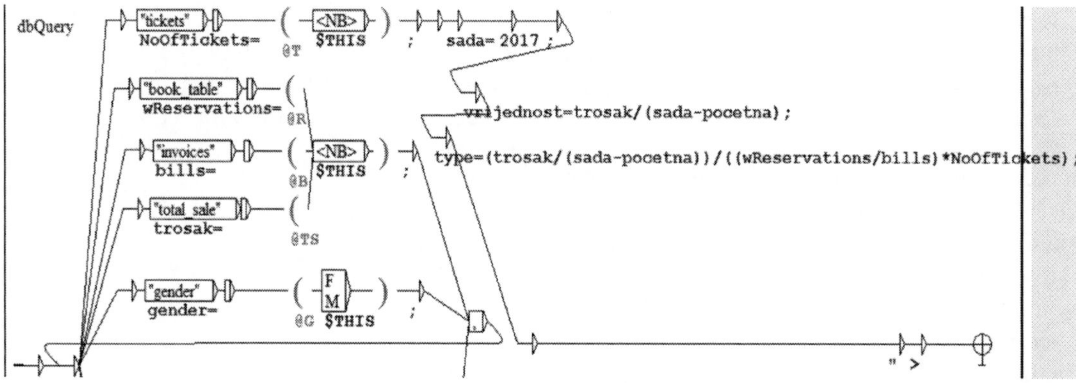

Figure 2: The *dbQuery* subgraph

For the purposes of our project[1], we were interested in the gender field {*gender*}, total amount of money spent since the first purchase {*trosak*}, total amount of invoices sent to the user since the first purchase {*bills*}, total amount of reservations made by the user via web {*wReservations*}, total number of tickets {*NoOfTickets*}.

Except for these fields, we needed to add present year {*sada*}, and formula for calculating the user's yearly average, i.e. how much s/he spends on tickets per year {*vrijednost*} and finally, formula for calculating the type of a user {*type*}. For the second formula, we considered how much money the user spends yearly, number of her/his web reservations, bills issued to the user and number of tickets actually bought. All the other database query results are recognized and annotated, but at this point, we are not using them in this project so they will not be further discussed.

In this grammar, we are using global variables (Silberztein, 2016) to ensure that our query results are available at all levels of the grammar i.e. in the main graph and also in all its subgraphs. We recognize them by the sign '@' used before the variable name. The most important one to us was the variable caring the gender value $@G since we needed this information in the following two sections to determine gender dependent forms of a noun, verb and pronoun, as we will show in the following paragraphs.

Within the subgraph [*user*] (Figure 3) we are introducing three new variables to determine the correct gender forms of a noun, verb and pronoun. The first variable $KO is given the value '*Korisnica*' (Eng. *she*-user) if the graph with the sub-grammar [F] is validated as true i.e. if the global variable $@G has the value set to feminine <$@G="F">. If the variable $@G has the value set to masculine <$@G="M"> then the variable $KO is given the value '*Korisnik*' (Eng. *he*-user).

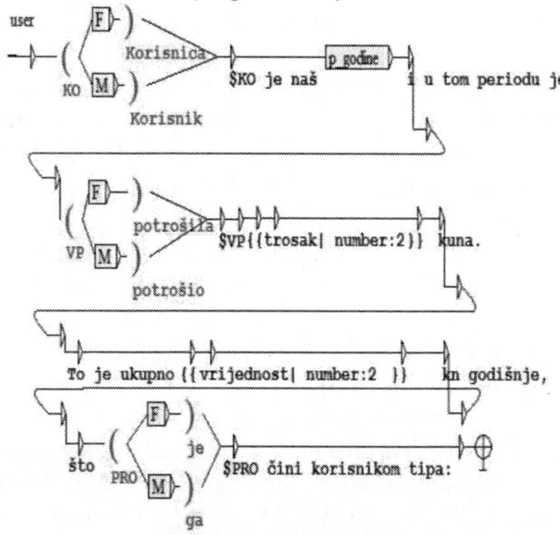

Figure 3: The subgraph *user*

The same validation is checked for the verb 'to spend' which takes the form '*potrošila*' or '*potrošio*' for the feminine and masculine user respectively, and for the accusative form of the pronouns 'she' and 'he' that become '*nju*' and '*ga*' in Croatian, depending on the gender. Since Croatian verbal past participles are gender dependent, we have used the constraint on customer's gender to produce the

[1] We believe that each agency will work with its own parameters that make up their types of different users. Parameters we chose here are for demonstration purposes only.

correct verb forms. If the constraint <$@G=”F”> is validated, NooJ takes the upper path and uses correct female forms of the main verb. Combination of gender constraints and tense operations allows us to generate correct sentences.

If all the validations check out correctly, there are two possible variants of this paragraph that can appear to the agent – one for the feminine (a) and one for the masculine user (b).

(a) ***Korisnica*** *je naš član X godina i u tom period je* ***potrošila*** *Y,00 kuna. To je ukupno Y,00 kn godišnje, što* ***nju*** *čini korisnikom tipa:* (Eng. **She-user** is our member for X years and in that period **she-spent** Y,00 kunas. That is a total of Y,00 kunas per year, which makes **her** a user of type:)

(b) ***Korisnik*** *je naš član X godina i u tom period je* ***potrošio*** *Y,00 kuna. To je ukupno Y,00 kn godišnje, što* ***ga*** *čini korisnikom tipa:* (Eng. **He-user** is our member for X years and in that period **he-spent** Y,00 kunas. That is a total of Y,00 kunas per year, which makes **him** a user of type:)

In the text, X and Y are replaced by the values calculated for each user in real time.

The *user* subgraph has one additional sub-grammar [*p_godine*] that checks for the number of years the user has been a customer (Figure 4). This check was necessary for two reasons:

- if our user is a new user, then s/he is described as a ‘*novi član*’ (Eng. new user) and we do not use the number of years to describe how long s/he has been the user. This way we have avoided awkward sentences like ‘*User has been our member for 0 years.*’ ;[2]
- for all the users that have been using the service for more than a year, we use the full number of years since s/he first used the services provided by the company. However, since the word for ‘year’ in Croatian changes its form depending on the number that precedes it, it was necessary to connect the proper number with the proper word form. Thus, if less than one year has passed since the first contact and today {*sad_poc*}, there are no years in between and we consider this person to be the new user. If the last digit is however greater than 0 and lower than 2, the word after the number {*god_clan*} takes the form ‘*godinu*’; if it is greater than 1 and lower than 5 it takes the form ‘*godine*’ and if it is greater than 4 it takes the form ‘*godina*’. Since NooJ does not support mathematical operations, in order to check the difference between the first contact and today, we moved these calculations to the web environment, but used NooJ to prepare the ground for all the possible calculations.

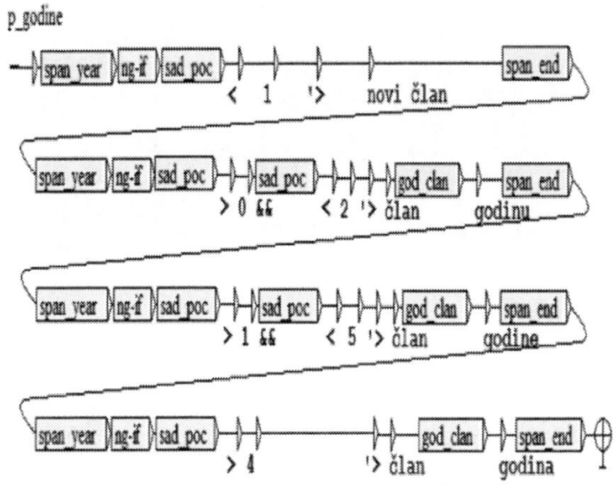

Figure 4: The subgraph *p_godine*

Similar check was performed in the final subgraph *Recommendations* (Figure 5).

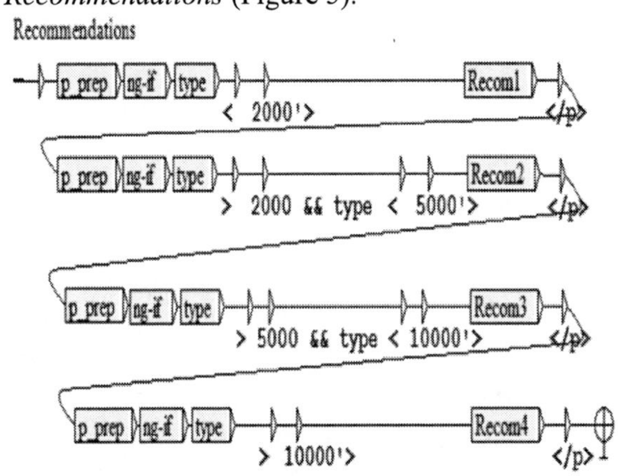

Figure 5: The subgraph *Recommendations*

In this subgraph we had to calculate the type of the user {*type*}, using the formula already prepared in the subgraph [*dbQuery*]. NooJ will again generate all four recommendations [*Recom1 .. Recom4*],

[2] Cf. section 2, examples 5,6 and 7.

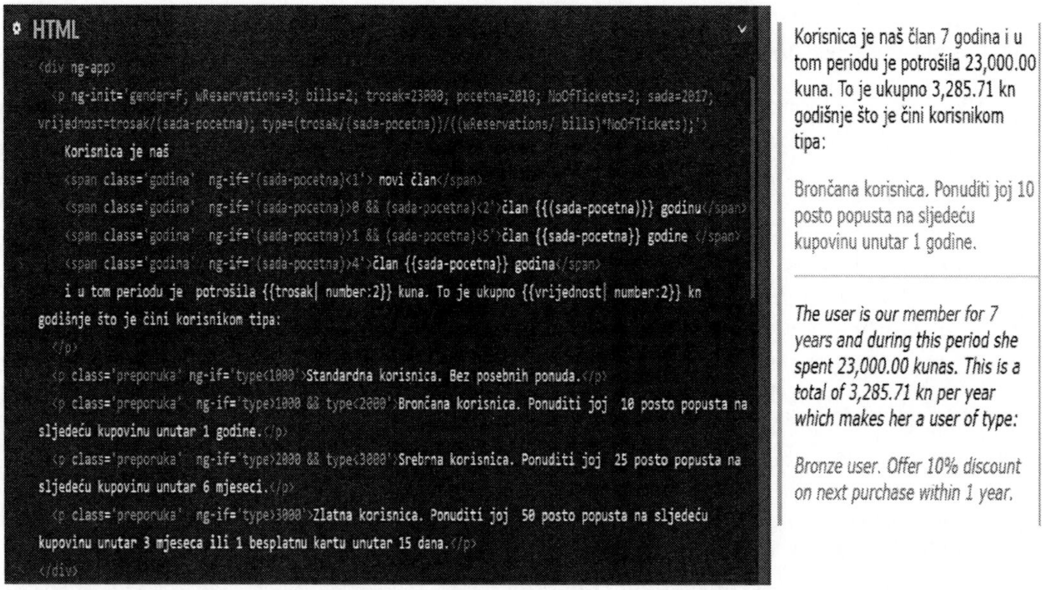

Figure 6: HTML code generated in NooJ (on the left) and its representation in a web viewer (on the right)

adopting them to the gender defined within the global variable $@G, while the final choice among offered recommendations will be performed within the web browser using the AngularJS.

Thus, depending on the gender, there are again two possible sets of recommendations that may be generated - (a) for the feminine and (b) for the masculine user:

(a) ***Recom1: Standardna korisnica.*** *Bez posebnih ponuda.* (Eng. ***She*-Standard user**. No special offers.)

Recom2: Brončana korisnica. *Ponuditi **joj** 10% popusta na sljedeću kupovinu unutar 1 godine.* (Eng. ***She*-Bronze user**. Offer **her** 10% discount on next purchase within 1 year.)

Recom3: Srebrna korisnica. *Ponuditi **joj** 25 % popusta na sljedeću kupovinu unutar 6 mjeseci.* (Eng. ***She*-Silver user**. Offer **her** 25% discount on next purchase within 6 months.)

Recom4: Zlatna korisnica. *Ponuditi **joj** 50% popusta na sljedeću kupovinu unutar 3 mjeseca ili 1 besplatnu kartu unutar 15 dana.* (Eng. ***She*-Golden user**. Offer **her** 50% discount on next purchase within 3 months or 1 free ticket within 15 days.)

(b) ***Recom1: Standardni korisnik.*** *Bez posebnih ponuda.* (Eng. ***He*-Standard user**. No special offers.)

Recom2: Brončani korisnik. *Ponuditi **mu** 10% popusta na sljedeću kupovinu unutar 1 godine.* (Eng. ***He*-Bronze user**. Offer **him** 10% discount on next purchase within 1 year.)

Recom3: Srebrni korisnik. *Ponuditi **mu** 25 % popusta na sljedeću kupovinu unutar 6 mjeseci.* (Eng. ***He*-Silver user**. Offer **him** 25% discount on next purchase within 6 months.)

Recom4: Zlatni korisnik. *Ponuditi **mu** 50% popusta na sljedeću kupovinu unutar 3 mjeseca ili 1 besplatnu kartu unutar 15 dana.* (Eng. ***He*-Golden user**. Offer **him** 50% discount on next purchase within 3 months or 1 free ticket within 15 days.).

5 Dealing with the control within the Web environment

There are several calculations that our project requires (number of years between user's first contact and today, user's average spending, type of the user depending on her/his spending…) in order to generate proper sentences. Since they could not be dealt with inside the NooJ environment, we have opted for AngularJS[3] that is considered to be "the most popular JavaScript MV (model view) solution in the world today" (Smith:Introduction, 2015). Its code allowed us to extend the HTML code with some new attributes that allow for JavaScript type functionality.

For this reason, it was necessary to incorporate all the needed AngularJS code in the text generated within NooJ. This is also the reason why all the text that depended on some mathematical calculations was generated and exported to the web environment where the final choice was made based upon the calculations (Figure 6).

The left side of Figure 6 shows the entire code prepared within NooJ, but notice that on the right side, not all generated parts of sentences[4] are shown. This was made possible by AngularJS part of the text. In fact, we gave Angular control over the <div> tag which holds our text. We constrained its scope only to this section of the page so it would not interfere with other frameworks used originally by the application.

6 Discussion and future work

We have demonstrated the procedure for a fast and straightforward recognition of customers' activities, their classification into various categories based on previous activities and the production of help messages for further interaction between a sales agent and a customer.

At this time, we have only considered situations when the user is a single private person, male or female. The problem of dealing with the company representatives still needs to be solved. But, if such a user can be distinguished within the database data, the grammar can adequately be extended with new sets of validations that will allow for the generation of new user specific descriptions and appropriate sets of recommendations.

In further work we intend to expand the algorithms used so far in order to enable predictions about future needs and desires of a customer. For example, if a customer regularly makes inquiries about flights and tickets using the web page interface, but the number of confirmed reservations is either decreasing or they are not realized at all, this can indicate that functionality of the web page is not satisfactory. This can also indicate that customers actually use web pages of other travel agencies for booking and purchase of air tickets.

Another line of research that we wish to pursue in the future is the generation of automatic reports for sales managers. These reports provide brief summarizations of all the activities recorded in the agent-customers interactions and enable quick changes or modifications of business strategies if necessary. By using NLG systems, the time required for the creation of such reports is shortened and it is possible to make quick decisions.

Further, such reports facilitate a better distribution of manpower, i.e. travel agents can direct their attention toward an individual client and her/his particular needs. For example, if the same customer makes online inquiries about flights without confirmation of reservation over several days, the system should alert a travel agent about these activities.

On the basis of these data, a sales agent can automatically generate an offer according to the parameters of the customer's search, using predefined textual samples. The intervention of sales agents in such cases would be minimal or even not necessary, since the system should be able to automatically make decisions and create offers in the form of short texts using the data stored in the database.

To sum up, a quality customer relationship management system nowadays should predict customers' wishes and needs and enable appropriate, efficient and quick actions.

7 Conclusion

This project presents the first steps in the natural language generation for Croatian in the domain of flight tickets. On the basis of data from a database

[3] https://angular.io/docs

[4] The English translation provided below the Croatian text is given here only for demonstrational purposes and is not part of the original project.

query, we are able to generate a text that gives an agent a quick summary of a customer with possible suggestions on how to proceed in her/his conduct. Such a quick insight should help agents make multi-criteria decisions faster and with more confidence, but within the business approved parameters. By producing natural language text that reduces the cognitive effort, agents can provide better service to their customers and thus upgrade the business results.

Acknowledgments

The authors wish to thank Travel Management Company d.o.o. for providing needed training data for this project.

References

Anabela Barreiro. 2008. ParaMT: a paraphraser for machine translation in *Lecture Notes in Computer Science,* vol. 5190, Springer-Verlag, pp 202-211.

John Bateman and Michael Zock. 2003. Natural Language Generation in *The Oxford Handook of Computational Linguistics* (ed. Ruslan Mitkov), Oxford University Press, pp 284-322.

Ines Boujelben, Slim Mesfar, Abdelmajid Ben Hamadou. 2012. Transformational Analysis of Arabic Sentences: Application to Automatically Extracted Biomedical Symptoms in *Automatic Processing of Various Levels of Linguistc Phenomena* (eds. K. Vučković, B. Bekavac, M. Silberztein), Newcastle upon Tyne: Cambridge Scholars Publishing, pp 182-194.

Albert Gatt and Emiel Krahmer. 2017. *Survey of the State of the Art in Natural Language Generation: Core tasks, applications and evaluation.* `https://arxiv.org/abs/1703.09902`. Date Accessed: May 27, 2017.

Daniel Jurafsky and James H. Martin. 2000. *Speech and Language Processing: An introduction to Natural Language Processing, Computational Linguistics, and Speech Recognition*, Prentice Hall, Upper Saddle River, New Jersey.

Rivindu Perera and Parma Nand. 2017. Recent Advances in Natural Language Generation: A Survey and Classification of the Empirical Literature. *Computing and Informatics,* Vol 36, No 1 (2017), pp 1-32.

Ehud Reiter and Robert Dale. 2000. *Building Natural Language Generation Systems*. Cambridge UP, Cambridge, UK.

Max Silberztein. 2012. Automatic Transformational Analysis and Generation in *Automatic Processing of Various Levels of Linguistc Phenomena* (eds. K. Vučković, B. Bekavac, M. Silberztein), Newcastle upon Tyne: Cambridge Scholars Publishing, pp 221-231.

Max Silberztein. 2016a. *Joe loves Lea:* Transformational Analysis of Direct Transitive Sentences in *Automatic Processing of Natural-Language Electronic Texts with NooJ. NooJ 2015* (eds. T. Okrut, Y. Hetsevich, M. Silberztein, H. Stanislavenka). Communications in Computer and Information Science, vol 607. Springer, Cham, pp 55-65.

Max Silberztein. 2016b. *Formalizing Natural Languages: The NooJ Approach,* Wiley. USA.

Chris Smith. 2015. *Angular Basics*. `http://www.angularjsbook.com/`. Date Accessed: May 11, 2017.

Jean-Sébastien Vayre, Estelle Delpech, Aude Dufresne and Céline Lemercier. 2017. Communication Mediated through Natural Language Generation in Big Data Environments: The Case of Nomao. *Journal of Computer and Communications,* 5, `https://doi.org/10.4236/jcc.2017.56008`, pp 125-148.

Simonetta Vietri 2012. Transformations and frozen sentences in *Automatic Processing of Various Levels of Linguistc Phenomena* (eds. K. Vučković, B. Bekavac, M. Silberztein), Newcastle upon Tyne: Cambridge Scholars Publishing, pp 166-180.

Using Electronic Dictionaries and NooJ to Generate Sentences Containing English Phrasal Verbs

Peter A. Machonis
Florida International University
Department of Modern Languages, Miami, FL 33199, USA
machonis@fiu.edu

Abstract

This paper attempts to explore NooJ's "generation" mode to automatically produce transformations of sentences containing English Phrasal Verbs (PV). We exploit the same electronic dictionary and grammar previously used to recognize PV in large corpora (Machonis 2010, 2012), but have had to design a specific grammar for generating sentences, following the examples in Silberztein (2016), which showed how NooJ could generate over two million transformations or parallel sentences from the simple sentence *Joe likes Lea*. We created a grammar that can generate variations of a single phrase containing one of the PV found in the NooJ PV dictionary. For the moment the grammar only handles singular nouns in the present and past tense, but it is capable of applying a succession of transformations – particle movement, preterit, negation, clefting, modal insertion, aspect introduction, question formation, and passive voice, along with various combinations of these transformations – to over 1,200 PV from the electronic dictionary.

1 Introduction

English Phrasal Verbs (PV) have presented a fascinating challenge for Natural Language Processing, and as we will see in this paper, for Automatic Natural Language Generation, as well. We used the NooJ platform, a freeware linguistic development environment that can be downloaded from http://www.nooj4nlp.net/. NooJ allows linguists to describe several levels of linguistic phenomena and then apply formalized descriptions to any corpus of texts. Previously, we have used NooJ to identify all PV in large corpora, such as the complete novels of Dickens and Melville, other 19th novels, as well as a transcribed oral corpus of *Larry King Live* programs from January 2000.

Hodapp (2010), however, is the only researcher who has used NooJ to recognize PV and then apply the results for language generation. Using the NooJ PV grammar and dictionary, she designed a graphical user interface to help undergraduate students reduce PV usage – often considered informal – in academic papers. Her program generated single-word verb suggestions that could take the place of automatically identified PV.

This paper attempts to explore NooJ's "generation" mode to automatically produce paraphrases of sentences that are described by grammars. We exploit the same electronic dictionary used in NooJ to recognize PV, but have had to design a specific grammar for generating sentences that involve PV. As an initial experiment, we created a grammar that can generate variations of a single phrase containing a PV, involving transformations such as particle movement, preterit, negation, clefting – both of the subject and the object – modal insertion, aspect introduction, question formation, and passive voice, along with various combinations of these transformations. For example, from one simple sentence, such as *Max figures out the problem*, NooJ can generate over 2,500 variations such as *Didn't Max figure out the problem?*, *It was Max who started to figure the problem out*, *He should figure it out*, etc.

2 NooJ's PV Parsing Capabilities

Using NooJ, Machonis (2010, 2012) showed that the automatic recognition of PV proved to be far more complex than for other multi-word expressions due to three main factors: (1) their possible discontinuous nature (e.g., ***let out*** *the dogs* ⇔ ***let*** *the dogs* ***out***), (2) their confusion with verbs followed by simple prepositions (e.g., *Do you remember what I* ***asked*** *you* ***in*** *Rome?* (preposition) vs. *Did you* ***ask***

Proceedings of the Linguistic Resources for Automatic Natural Language Generation Workshop, pages 33–37, Santiago de Compostela, Spain, September 4, 2017.

the prince ***in*** *when he arrived?* (PV)), and (3) genuine ambiguity only resolvable from context (e.g., *Her neighbor was* ***looking over*** *the broken fence*, which can mean either "looking above the fence" (preposition) or "examining the fence" (PV)). On the bright side, though, NooJ can correctly identify many discontinuous PV, such as the following:

(1) I **folded** all my bills **up** uniformly (*Great Expectations*)

(2) he had that club-hammer there ... to **knock** some one's brains **out** with (*Moby Dick*)

(3) a program that has effectively **brought** our crime rates **down** (*Larry King Live*).

NooJ requires both a grammar and a dictionary that work in tandem to annotate PV in large corpora. Figure 1 represents an example of NooJ's PV Grammar.

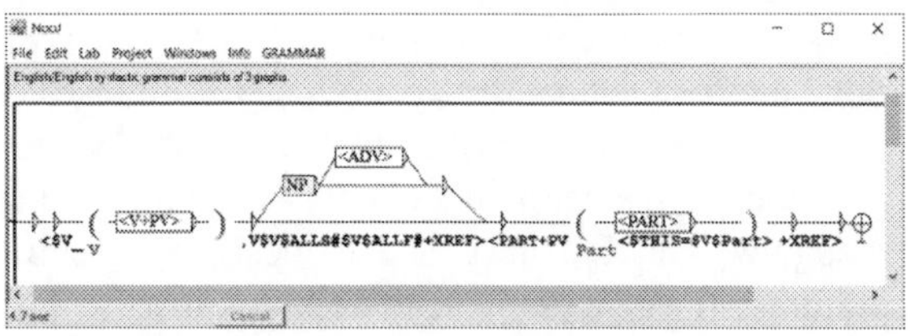

Figure 1: NooJ PV Grammar

The dictionary is based on previous work using Maurice Gross' (1994, 1996) Lexicon-Grammar approach. Lexicon-Grammar limits abstract notions in syntax and accentuates the reproducibility of linguistic data in the form of exhaustive syntactic tables, which are manually constructed and contain both lexical and syntactic information, as can be seen in the sample Table 1. From these Lexicon-Grammar tables of PV, we created a NooJ PV dictionary that contains more than 1,200 entries, which when used in tandem with the PV grammar, could automatically annotate PV in large corpora. Figure 2 is a sample of this dictionary, which mirrors much of the information contained within the Lexicon-Grammar entry seen in Table 1.

Although early experiments identified much noise, three disambiguation grammars, adverbial and adjectival expression filters, and idiom dictionaries were added to remove false PV without creating silence. This has made for a fairly intricate way to accurately annotate PV in large corpora. Machonis (2016) explains how NooJ can successfully remove many inaccurate Text Annotation Structures (TAS).

N_0 =: Nhum	N_0 =: N-hum	Verb	Particle	Example of N_1	N_1 =: Nhum	N_1 =: N-hum	N_0 V N_1	N_1 V Part	N_1 V	Synonym
+	+	beef	up	the proposal	-	+	-	-	-	strengthen
+	+	bend	up	the credit card	-	+	+	-	-	bend completely
+	-	bind	up	the wound	+	+	+	-	-	bandage
+	+	block	up	the sink	-	+	+	+	-	obstruct
+	+	blow	up	the balloons	-	+	-	-	-	inflate
+	+	blow	up	the building	+	+	-	+	+	explode
+	+	blow	up	the photo	-	+	-	-	-	enlarge
+	+	blow	up	the scandal	-	+	-	+	-	exaggerate
+	-	boil	up	some water	-	+	+	-	+	boil

Table 1: Sample from PV Lexicon-Grammar

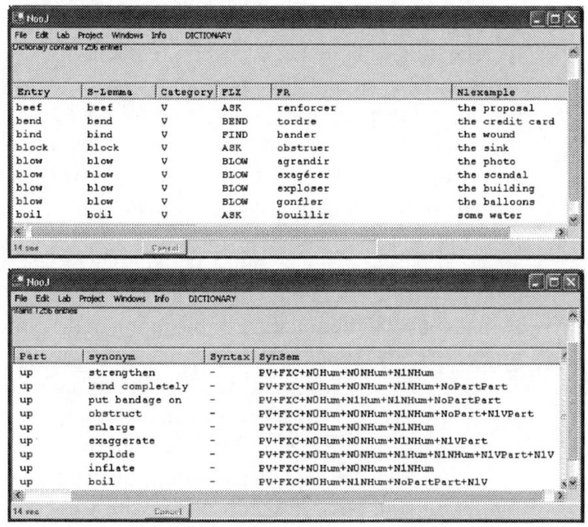

Figure 2: NooJ PV Dictionary

Overall, our NooJ PV studies have achieved 88% accuracy, with most of the noise coming from the particles *in* and *on*, which are fairly tricky to distinguish automatically from prepositions (e.g. ***had*** *a strange smile* ***on*** *her thin lips* (preposition) vs. ***had*** *her hat and jacket* ***on*** (PV)). However, in a more recent study on the novels of Dickens and Melville, we reduced the NooJ dictionary to include only six particles (*out*, *up*, *down*, *away*, *back*, *off*) instead of twelve, which helped us achieve 98% accuracy. Other linguists, such as Hiltunen (1994:135), also limited searches to these six typical particles representing three levels of PV frequency: high (*out*, *up*), mid (*down*, *away*), and low (*back*, *off*). However, for our generation study, we used the original PV dictionary of over 1,200 entries.

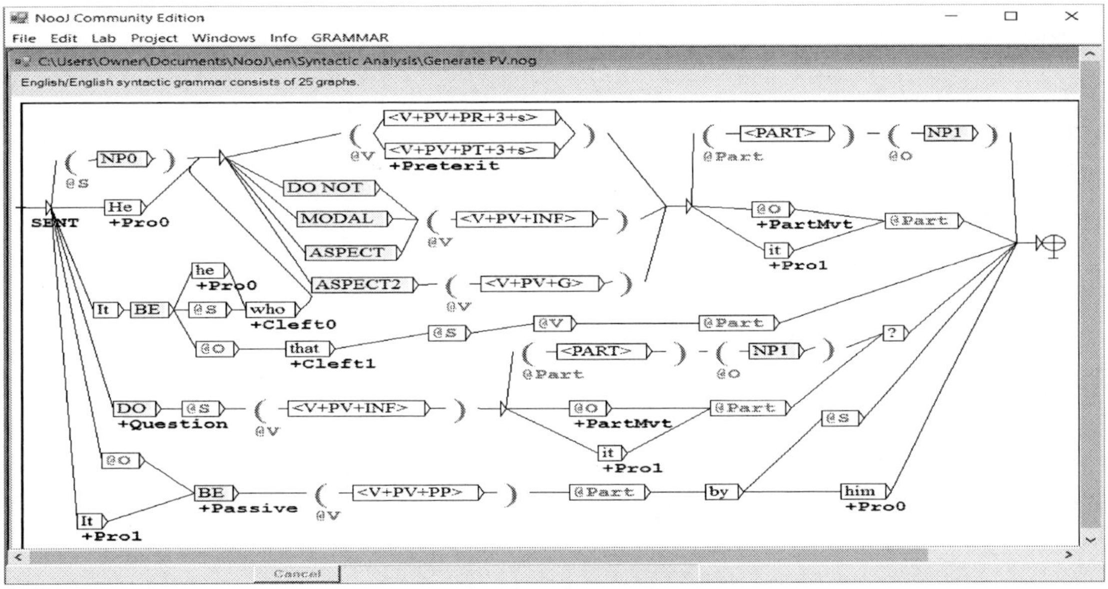

Figure 3: NooJ PV Generate Grammar

3 NooJ's PV Generating Capabilities

As an initial experiment, we created a grammar that can generate variations of a single phrase containing a PV. We changed the local variables in the original PV parsing grammar to global variables, and then added new pathways for the various transformations, following the examples in Silberztein (2015, 2016), which showed how NooJ could generate over two million transformations or parallel sentences from simple sentences, such as *Luc aime Léa* 'Luke likes Lea' and *Joe likes Lea.*

For the moment the grammar (Figure 3) only handles singular nouns in the present and past tense, but it is capable of applying a succession of transformations – particle movement, preterit, negation, clefting (both of the subject and the object), modal insertion, aspect introduction, question formation, and passive voice – to over 1,200 PV from the electronic dictionary. The upper pathway recognizes a sentence containing a PV and creates the first variants, with past tense and particle movement. So, if we enter: *Max figures out the problem*, that sentence is recognized, but NooJ also creates, *Max figured out the problem*, *Max figures the problem out*, and *Max figured the problem out*. Also, *Max* and *the problem* could be substituted by pronouns.

The next series of transformations deal with negation, modal insertion and aspect introduction. These pathways create variations such as *Max did not figure out the problem*, *Max could figure out the problem*, *Max started to figure the problem out*, *Max finished figuring out the problem*, etc. Our modal subgraph includes nine modal verbs – *can*, *could*, *may*, *might*, *must*, *should*, *ought to*, *need to*, *have to* -- as well as negative variants and contracted forms, such as *can't*, *shouldn't*, etc. Our aspectual variants include inchoative (*begin*, *start*), durative (*continue*), and completive (*finish*, *stop*), with both negative and preterit possibilities.

In the middle of the graph, we have the clefting conduit, either *It is he who*, *It is Max who*, or *It is the problem that*, followed by the same PV. In the case of clefting of the subject, the sentence will also undergo particle movement, negation, modal insertion, and aspectual variants. Thus sentences such as the following would be created: *It was Max who didn't figure it out*, *It is Max who may not figure the problem out*, *It was Max who started to figure the problem out*, *It was Max who didn't finish figuring it out*, etc.

The final two pathways involve question formation and passive voice formation: *Does Max figure out the problem?* and *The problem is figured out by Max*. These variants are also open to negative and preterit transformations, along with pronominal forms, such as: *Didn't Max figure it out?*, *The problem was not figured out by him*, etc.

Bob figured the problem out	SENT+Preterit+PartMvt
Bob has to figure it out	SENT+ModHave+Pro1
It is Bob who could figure out the problem	SENT+Cleft0+ModCan+Preterit
Mike must clear away the area	SENT+ModMust
Mike needn't clear the area away	SENT+ModNeed+Neg+Contraction+PartMvt
Mike oughtn't clear it away	SENT+ModOught+Neg+Contraction+Pro1
Brent continued to push the deadline back	SENT+Preterit+AspDurative+PartMvt
Didn't Brent push the deadline back ?	SENT+Question+Preterit+Neg+Contraction+PartMvt
It is not he who pushed the deadline back	SENT+Neg+Pro0+Cleft0+Preterit+PartMvt
Did Blake hand the exam in ?	SENT+Question+Preterit+PartMvt
He handed it in	SENT+Pro0+Preterit+Pro1
It wasn't Blake who handed in the exam	SENT+Preterit+Neg+Contraction+Cleft0+Preterit
Phil might call off the trip	SENT+ModMay+Preterit
Phil started to call the trip off	SENT+Preterit+AspInchoative+PartMvt
It isn't Phil who called it off	SENT+Neg+Contraction+Cleft0+Preterit+Pro1
Steve started turning on the radio,	SENT+Preterit+AspInchoative
Steve began to turn the radio on,	SENT+Preterit+AspInchoative+PartMvt
It wasn't Steve who didn't turn the radio on	SENT+Preterit+Neg+Contraction+Cleft0+Preterit+Neg+Contraction+PartMvt
Max couldn't burn the building down	SENT+ModCan+Preterit+Neg+Contraction+PartMvt
Max stops burning down the building	SENT+AspCompletive
The building wasn't burnt down by Max	SENT+Passive+Preterit+Neg+Contraction
Didn't Devon shred the document up ?	SENT+Question+Preterit+Neg+Contraction+PartMvt
Did Devon shred it up ?	SENT+Question+Preterit+Pro1
It isn't Devon who couldn't shred it up	SENT+Neg+Contraction+Cleft0+ModCan+Preterit+Neg+Contraction+Pro1

Table 2: Sample Sentences from NooJ PV Generate Grammar with Transformations Noted

All in all, for every sentence containing a PV, this NooJ grammar will create 2,694 entries, and sometimes more in the case of certain irregular verbs, such as *burn*, which has two past tenses, *burned* and *burnt*. This grammar can also generate sentences based on all the other PV in the NooJ PV dictionary such as, *clear away the area*, *push back the deadline*, *hand in the exam*, *call off the trip*, *turn on the radio*, *burn down the building*, *shred up the document*, etc. as can be seen in Table 2. If we apply the PV Generate Grammar to all of the 1,200 verbs listed in the NooJ PV dictionary, NooJ would have generated over three million different sentences.

4 Conclusion

Not only does this research shed light on a major NLG problem, i.e., generating sentences containing discontinuous multiword expressions, but it seems to approach solving the original Chomskian challenge of generating "all and only" the sentences of a language. Some of these sentences might sound more natural than others, and some will need a specific context to appear likely, however, all of the sentences generated are grammatical. Speakers may choose certain forms over others during the course of a conversation, in what might be called discourse management. Nevertheless, NooJ does allow the user to specify which transformations are to be applied and thus limit the number of sentences generated to a specific context. As can be seen in this preliminary test, NooJ is a very powerful tool for linguistics, as well as Natural Language Generation.

References

Maurice Gross. 1994. Constructing Lexicon-Grammars. *Computational Approaches to the Lexicon* (eds. Atkins and Zampolli), 213-263. Oxford University Press, Oxford, UK

Maurice Gross. 1996. Lexicon Grammar. *Concise Encyclopedia of Syntactic Theories* (eds. K. Brown and J. Miller), 244-258. Elsevier, New York.

Risto Hiltunen. 1994. On Phrasal Verbs in Early Modern English: Notes on Lexis and Style. *Studies in Early Modern English* (ed. D. Kastovsky), 129-140. Mouton de Gruyter, Berlin, Germany.

Lien Huynh Hodapp. 2010. *Eliminating phrasal verbs in academic writing*. Minnesota State University Memorial Library University Archives, Mankato, Minnesota.

Peter A. Machonis. 2010. English Phrasal Verbs: from Lexicon-Grammar to Natural Language Processing. *Southern Journal of Linguistics* 34(1): 21-48.

Peter A. Machonis. 2012. *Sorting* NooJ *out* to *take* Multiword Expressions *into account. Automatic Processing of Various Levels of Linguistic Phenomena: Selected Papers from the NooJ 2011 International Conference* (eds K. Vučković, B. Bekavac, and M. Silberztein), 152-165. Cambridge Scholars Publishing, Newcastle upon Tyne, UK.

Peter A. Machonis. 2016. Phrasal Verb Disambiguating Grammars: Cutting Out Noise Automatically. *Automatic Processing of Natural-Language Electronic Texts with NooJ. Communications in Computer and Information Science book series (CCIS, volume 667),* (eds L. Barone, M. Monteleone and M. Silberztein). 169-181. Springer International Publishing AG, Cham, Switzerland.

Max Silberztein. 2015. *La formalisation des langues: l'approache de NooJ*. ISTE Editions, London,UK.

Max Silberztein. 2016. *Formalizing Natural Languages: The NooJ Approach*. Wiley ISTE, London,UK.

Generating Text with Correct Verb Conjugation: Proposal for a New Automatic Conjugator with NooJ

Héla Fehri, Sondes Dardour
MIRACL Laboratory, University of Sfax
hela.fehri@yahoo.fr, dardour.sondes@yahoo.com

Abstract

This paper describes a system that generates texts with correct verb conjugation. The proposed system integrates a conjugator developed using a linguistic approach. This latter is based on dictionaries and transducers built with the NooJ linguistic platform. The conjugator treats three languages: Arabic, French and English. It recognizes all verbs and allows their conjugation in different tenses. The results obtained are satisfactory and can easily be improved upon by processing other forms, such as the negative.

1 Introduction

Automatic Language Processing is an area of multidisciplinary research that permits the collaboration of linguists, computer scientists, logicians, psychologists, documentalists, lexicographers, and translators.

In this domain different conjugators are built and used (Rello and Basterrechea, 2010). The term conjugation is applied only to the inflection of verbs, and not to other parts of speech (inflection of nouns and adjectives is known as declension). The development of the conjugator is not an easy task and depends on the specificities of the processed language. Among existing conjuagators, for Arabic, we can cite *AlKanz*[1] and *qutrub*[2]. For the French language, we find *Le Figaro*[3] and *Reverso Conjugaison*[4]. And for English, we can cite The conjugator[5], conjugation.com and *Reverso Conjugaison*[6]. The difference between these conjugators lies in the number of languages, forms (negative, interrogative) and voices processed. They can be in different forms such as a website or mobile application.

The aim of this paper is to *generate* a text with well-conjugated verbs. To reach this objective, we propose to develop a system that allows parsing a text, extracting different infinitive forms of verbs and conjugate them in the appropriate tense. This system integrates a conjugator, which makes it possible to conjugate Arabic, French, and English verbs in the desired tense. This conjugator should guarantee the correct conjugation of verbs without errors.

In this paper, after an introduction to the proposed method, we describe our resource construction and implementation using the NooJ linguistic platform (Silberztein and Tutin, 2005). Then, we give an idea of the experimentation and the results obtained and conclude with some future perspectives.

2 Proposed Method

As shown in Figure 1, the proposed method requires four steps or two phases: the identification, construction and compilation of resources phase and the conjugation phase in which the conjugator of verbs is integrated. In what follows, we will examine each phase in detail.

2.1 Identification, construction and compilation of resources

The step of constructing and compiling resources consists in identifying the lexical resources represented by dictionaries and building the syntactic grammars represented by transducers.

[1] http://www.al-kanz.org/2007/06/26/conjugaison-arabe/
[2] https://qutrub.arabeyes.org/
[3] http://leconjugueur.lefigaro.fr/
[4] http://conjugueur.reverso.net/conjugaison-francais.html
[5] http://www.theconjugator.com/
[6] http://conjugueur.reverso.net/conjugaison-anglais.html

Proceedings of the Linguistic Resources for Automatic Natural Language Generation Workshop, pages 39–42, Santiago de Compostela, Spain, September 4, 2017.

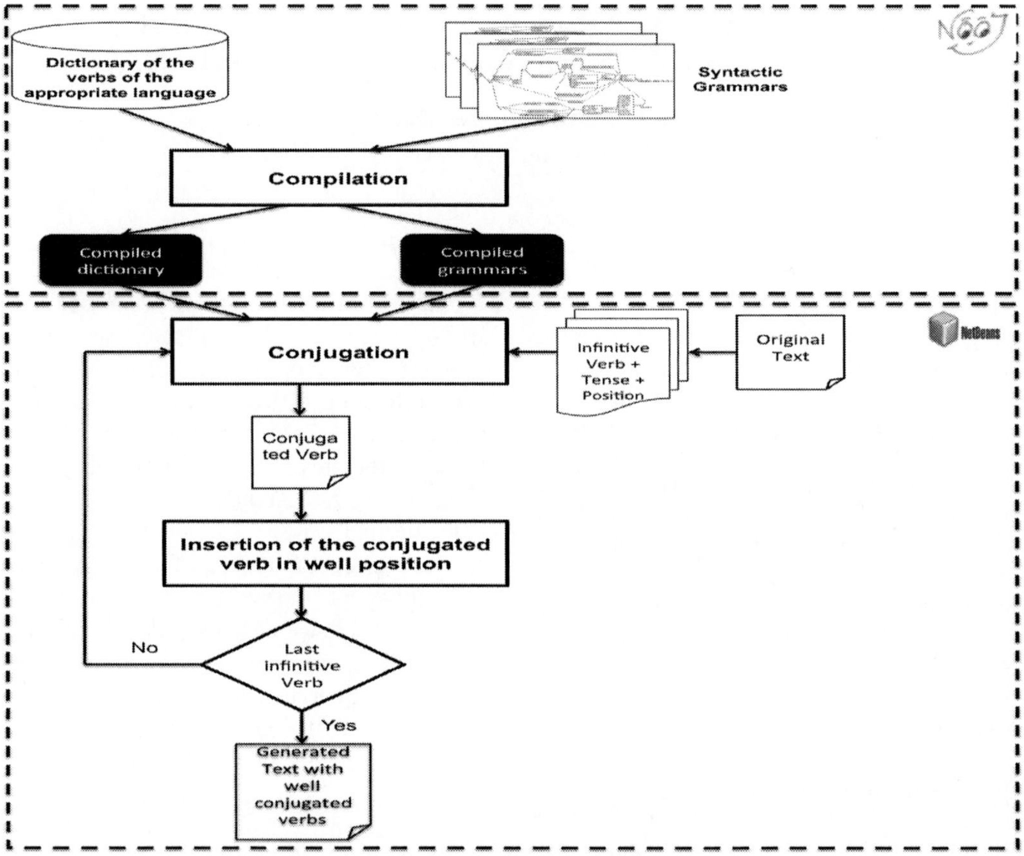

Figure 1: Proposed method

Identification of dictionaries: A NooJ dictionary is an electronic dictionary designed for use by computer systems. A NooJ dictionary contains different entries. The structure of an entry is specific to each dictionary, but contains at least the grammatical category of the entry (Name, Adjective, Verb, etc.).

In our work, we use three dictionaries: the dictionary of Arabic verbs (verbes arabes.nod) which contains 9,257 entries (Fehri et al., 2016), the dictionary of French verbs (_dm.nod) which contains 67,983 entries (Trouilleux, 2011) and the dictionary of English verbs (_sdic.nod) which contains 90,000 entries (Silberztein, 2003).

Each dictionary contains a derivation module to recognize the derived forms and a flexional module to recognize the inflected forms of the verb.

Construction of grammars: A grammar is a set of graphs. The number of grammars depends on the number of tenses treated to perform the conjugation. Note that each language has its proper tenses.

For Arabic, we have processed four tenses: the past tense (أَلْمَاضِي *al-māḍī*), the present tense (أَلْمُضَارِع *al-muḍāri'*), the future tense and the imperative (اَلْأَمْر *al-amr*). Figure 2 represents the conjugation of the verbs in the future (F) with different Arabic pronouns.

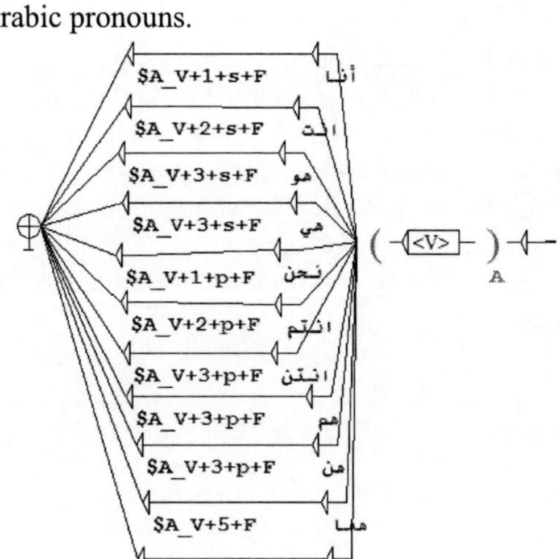

Figure 2: Conjugation of verbs in the future

For French, we have treated all tenses (present, past and future), aspects (perfective and imperfective), as well as all moods (indicative, imperative, subjunctive, conditional and gerundive). Figure 3 describes the conjugation of verbs in the present tense (PR) (tense: present, mood: indicative).

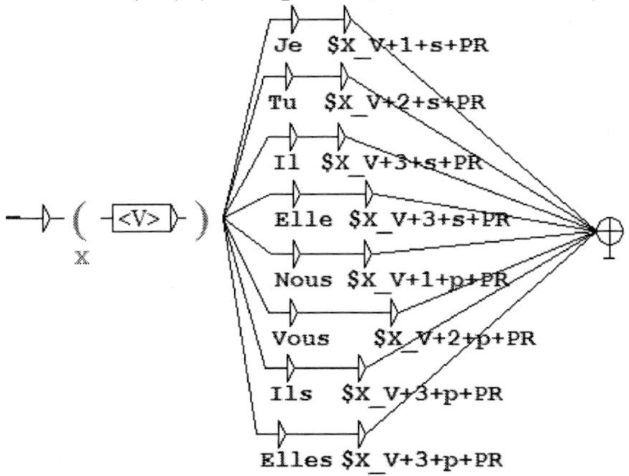

Figure 3: Conjugation of verbs in the present tense

For English, we have processed all possible combinations of tense, aspect and mood: present tenses (simple present and continuous present), past tenses (simple past and continuous past), present perfect tenses (present perfect (simple) and present perfect (continuous)), past perfect tenses (past perfect (simple) and past perfect (continuous)) and future tenses (simple future, continuous future, future perfect (simple) and future perfect (continuous)). Figure 4 describes the conjugation of verbs in the simple past (PT) with all pronouns.

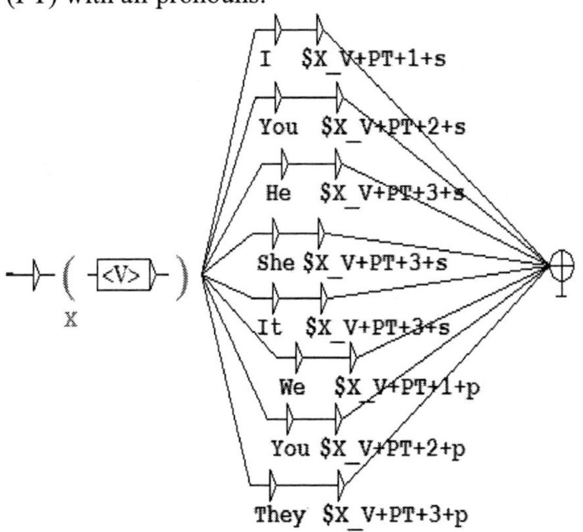

Figure 4: Conjugation of verbs in the past

Compilation of resources: The compilation phase consists of generating grammars and dictionaries in binary format that can be exploited in a later step.

2.2 Conjugation of verbs

The conjugation of verbs is done in three steps: parsing of the text, extraction of the infinitive form, its position and the desired tense, and conjugation of the extracted verb in the appropriate language. In our case, verbs to be conjugated and tenses are delimited by special characters such as parentheses.

To conjugate a verb, we use compiled resources described in section 2.1. Theses resources are used with command-line program *noojapply*, which is accessed from Java. Once the verb is conjugated, it will be inserted in the correct position in the generated text. The three steps mentioned will be repeated until processing of all verbs to be conjugated in the original text is complete.

3 Experimentation and evaluation

The experimentation of our system is done using NooJ and Java. As mentioned above, NooJ uses syntactic and morphological grammars already built. To evaluate our work, we have applied our resources to 300 texts in different languages: Arabic, French and English. Figure 5 represents an excerpt of results obtained when applying our system to an English text.

As shown in Figure 5, our system gives satisfactory results. However, some problems are related to the lack of standards for writing verbs (e.g., the hamza) in Arabic and the difficulties of dealing with some forms, such as the negative and interrogative forms and the passive voice.

Table 1 gives an idea about tenses and verbs processed by our system.

	Languages		
	Arabic	French	English
Number of tenses	4	17	12
Number of verbs	9 257	67 983	90 000

Table 1: Description of the conjugator.

Note that the number of verbs indicated in Table 1 represents only the lemmas that exist in our dictionary. The derived forms are also recognized by our system thanks to morphological grammars.

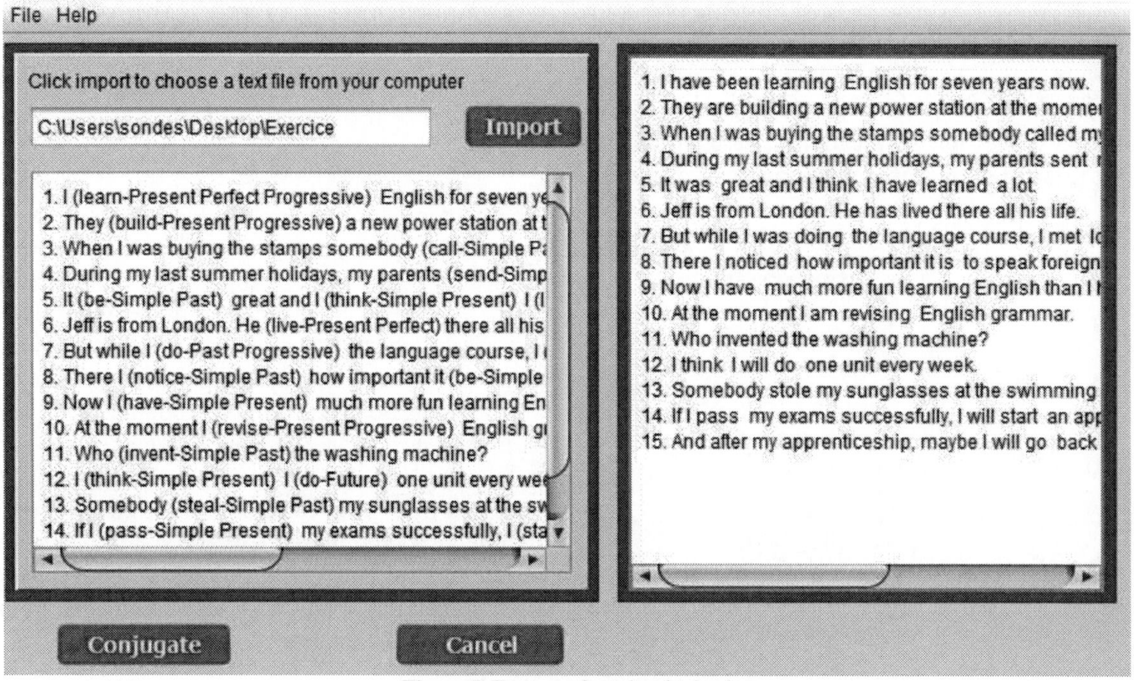

Figure 5: Excerpt of results obtained

4 Conclusion

The system we developed helps to learn how to conjugate a verb correctly. It can be used as a teaching tool for learning conjugation. It gives also sufficient results.

In the future, we aim to improve the conjugator by processing other forms (interrogative and negative) and the passive voice. Furthermore, we want to add other concepts and rules in order to know the tense of the verb without indicating it. This is possible by examining the context of the sentence.

References

Hela Fehri, Mohamed Zaidi and Kamel Boudhina. 2016. *Création d'un dictionnaire des verbes NooJ open source pour la langue arabe*. Report of the end of studies project. Higher Institute of Management of Gabes

Luz Rello and Eduardo Basterrechea. 2010. Automatic conjugation and identification of regular and irregular verb neologisms in Spanish, *Proceedings of the NAACL HLT 2010 Second Workshop on Computational Approaches to Linguistic Creativity*, pp 1–5, Los Angeles, California, June 2010.

Max Silberztein. 2003. *NooJ Manual* Available for download at: www.nooj4nlp.net.

Max Silberztein and Agnès Tutin. 2005. NooJ, un outil TAL pour l'enseignement des langues. *Application pour l'étude de la morphologie lexicale en FLE*. Special Atala, 8(2), pp 123-34.

François Trouilleux. 2011. *Le DM*, A French dictionary for NooJ. In *Automatic Processing of Various Levels of Linguistic Phenomena: Selected Papers from the NooJ 2011 International Conference* (eds. K. Vučković, B. Bekavac and M. Silberztein). Cambridge Scholars Publishing, pp 16-28.

Formalization of Speech Verbs with NooJ for Machine Translation: the French Verb accuser

Jouda Ghorbel
Language Laboratory and Automatic Processing, University of Sfax, Tunisia
joudaghorbel@yahoo.fr

Abstract

The mediocrity of sentences generated by online translators (Jacqueline, 1998; Hutchins, 2001) prompts us to try to find a solution to have more reliable translations. This is a very difficult task due to the ambiguity of natural languages and especially the deficiencies of translation systems in terms of syntactic and semantic knowledge. How can we make automatic translation more reliable and unambiguous? Our main objective will be to generate a text where the translation of French verbs into Arabic will be without ambiguities. In this contribution, we attempt to formalize a particular class of verbs, namely the so-called verbs of speech. We shall limit ourselves to the treatment of the verb *accuser* 'to accuse' as presented in the Dubois & Dubois-Charlier (1997) electronic dictionary, *Les verbes français*. We shall take this verb as a prototype to show how NooJ can perform a reliable machine translation and generate a good text without ambiguities.

1 Introduction

The process of creating translation machines, capable of properly translating verbs, takes place in two stages: a theoretical stage and an application stage. The first phase allows analyzing and interpreting the phenomena studied which is then developed in the second phase whose role is to produce an automatic translation. In this contribution, we will try to automatically treat a class of verbs, namely the so-called verbs of speech. To do this we have adopted the NooJ platform for the syntactic description of the French verb *accuser* 'to accuse' as an example of speech verbs. Our two main objectives, which are in the realm of applied linguistics, include:

- The production of a system of analysis and recognition of the syntactic patterns of the verb *accuser* according to the classification of French verbs.
- An adequate and reliable machine translation and the generation of sentences into Arabic.

Our work will therefore be divided into four parts: Derivational and inflectional formalization;

Syntactic formalization;

Implementation of the verb *accuser* in NooJ for machine translation;

Automatic translation and generation of sentences in Arabic.

2 Derivational and inflectional formalization

The NooJ software has its own tools for automatic verb analysis and processing (Silberztein, 2003), so we need to formalize the linguistic data, in order that the program can automatically analyze and process the verb *accuser* in all of its various shades of meaning in our corpus, and then accurately translate them.

We will therefore create the necessary paradigms to link each derivative or verb conjugated to its infinitive form.

2.1 Creation of derivational paradigms

We have chosen our verb example from Dubois & Dubois-Charlier's (1997) electronic dictionary, *Les verbes français* (LVF). This work presents derivational codes which can be adjectival, such as

Proceedings of the Linguistic Resources for Automatic Natural Language Generation Workshop, pages 43–47, Santiago de Compostela, Spain, September 4, 2017.

in *–able* and *–ant*, or nominal derivations, as in *-age*, *–ment*, *–ion*, *–eur*, *and –ure.*

The verb *accuser* in the LVF has only one nominal derivative: *accusateur* 'accuser', we have created in NooJ its paradigm that we called

N1 = *accuser*<B2> *ateur* / N.

The LVF dictionary clearly indicated the different derivatives for each verb, but their inflections were not mentioned in the feminine nor in the plural, so we had to create these inflectional paradigms so that NooJ could recognize the inflected derivative forms: *accusateur* = <E> / m + s | s / m + p | <B3> *rice* / f s + | <B3> *rices* / f + p.

2.2 Creation of inflectional paradigms

NooJ will automatically be able to recognize the conjugated forms of a verb only when describing the conjugation models indicated in LVF with the NooJ inflectional operators. For that, Max Silberztein[1] matched the conjugation codes of NooJ.

Example: the verb *aimer* 'to love' is inflected as:

```
Aimer   =    <E>/INF      |    <B2>ant/G       |
      <B2>é/PP+m+s  | <B2>ée/PP+f+s        |
      <B2>és/PP+m+p  | <B2>ées/PP+f+p      |
      <B>/IP+s+2    |   <B2>ons/IP+p+1     |
      <B>z/IP+p+2   |   <B>/PR+s+1         |
      <B>s/PR+s+2     |     <B>/PR+s+3     |
      <B2>ons/PR+p+1   |   <B>z/PR+p+2     |
      <B>nt/PR+p+3     |     <B>/S+s+1     |
      <B>s/S+s+2      |     <B>/S+s+3      |
      <B2>ions/S+p+1  | <B2>iez/S+p+2      |
      <B>nt/S+p+3      |     ais/C+s+1     |
      ais/C+s+2       |     ait/C+s+3      |
      ions/C+p+1      |     iez/C+p+2      |
      aient/C+p+3.
```

For this inflectional paradigm of the verb *aimer* all the tenses, and moods have been described with all the personal pronouns using NooJ operators and thanks to this model we can conjugate a large number of verbs, such as *accuser* our example verb.

NooJ can now recognize all the conjugated occurrences of the verb *accuser* in our corpus, lemmatize them and link them to the list of the various uses.

3 Syntactic formalization

In this phase, we describe the syntactic schemas, which are written in the form of codes, replace the codes with the verb and its arguments, and assign them semantic features based on their syntactic schemas. Syntactic schemas are defined by the nature of the constituents of the sentence, their properties and their relations, and by the words of the lexicon which enter into the various types of constituents.

a. *Accuser* direct transitive verb

- **[T11b0]** CONS = T11b0 + N0VN1PREPN2 + N0Hum + V + N1Hum + N2Abst + N2Vinf + PREP = « de »

  Ex: *La mère accuse son enfant d'avoir oublié ses devoirs.* 'The mother reproaches her child for having forgotten her homework'.

- **[T1907]** CONS = N0VN1 Nhum + VT + N1Hum N1Abst+ N1Conc

  Ex: *On accuse le sort.* 'We accuse fate'.

b. *Accuser* pronominal verb

- **[P10B0]** CONS = N0seVPREPN1 + N0Hum + VP + N1Hum + N1Abst + N1Vinf + PREP ="de"

  Ex*: L'enfant s'accuse d'avoir menti* 'The child reproaches himself for having lied'.

After this phase of derivational, inflectional and syntactic formalization of the verb *accuser* with NooJ operators, we proceed to the implementation of these formal data within NooJ.

4 Implementation of the verb *accuser* in NooJ for automatic translation

In this phase of formalization we show how to integrate the verbal input *accuser* in NooJ for automatic translation. For this, we created a bilingual French Arabic dictionary and formal grammars for the different constructions of the verb *accuser*.

[1] Author of the software NooJ

4.1 Creation of a bilingual Arabic dictionary

This phase of implementation of the verb in a bilingual French-Arabic dictionary aims first of all to reformulate the information of the LVF in terms of NooJ operators. This operation consists of applying the dictionary to automatically translate the text into Arabic. We added the Arabic translation to each verb and all the other words in order to generate sentences into Arabic without ambiguities.

In this phase, we reformulate the information of the LVF in connection with the verb *accuser* and apply this dictionary to the French-Arabic machine translation (Figure 1).

```
Accuser,
V+COM+AUX=AVOIR+FLX=AIMER
+CONS=T11b0+N0VN1PREPN2+N0Hum
+V+N1Hum+PREP="de"+N2Abst+Vinf
+CONS=B10b0+N0seVPREPN1+N0Hum
+V+PREP="de"+N1Abst+Vinf
+Sens=reprocher à+AR="تلوم"

Accuser,
V+COM+AUX=AVOIR+FLX=AIMER
+CONS=T1907+N0VN1+N0Hum
+V+N1Hum+N1Abst
+Sens= invectiver+AR="ادان"

criminel,N+FLX=S_DE+AR="المجرم"
juge,N+FLX=S_0+AR="القاضي
mère,N+FLX=F_S+AR="الام"
enfant,N+FLX=S_0+AR="ابنها"
courir,V+FLX=COURIR+AR="الركض"
de,PREP+AR="على"
mentir,V+FLX=SENTIR+AR="الكذب"
```

Figure 1: Excerpt from the dictionary accuser.dic

4.2 The creation of formal grammars for the different constructions of the verb *accuser*

For a reliable automatic translation of sentences containing the verb *accuser,* we tried to create formal grammars (Figure 2 for T11b0 and P10b0 constructions; Figure 3 for T1907 construct) to remove the ambiguities of the various syntactic constructions.

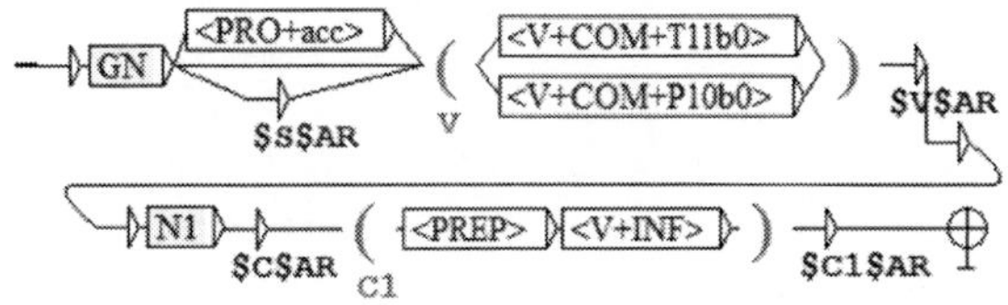

Figure 2: The formal grammars of the constructions T11b0 and P10b0.

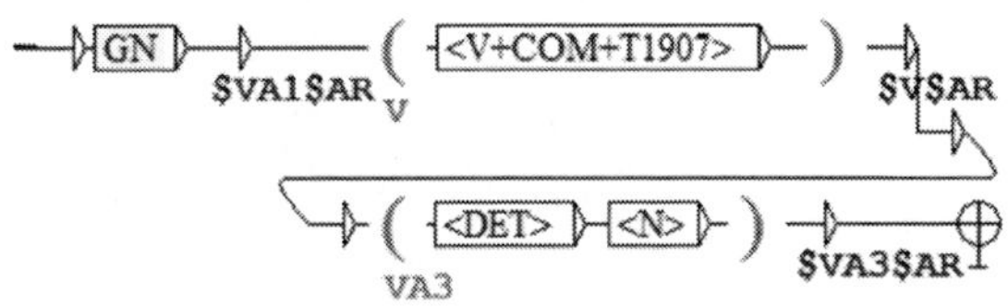

Figure 3: The formal grammars of the construction T1907

Boons et al. (1976) claim that the meaning of the verb is related to the type of subject and the complement (human, concrete, non-animated, etc.); we created formal grammars that take into consideration the type of the object and the type of the complement. The verb *accuser* has three different syntactic constructs: T11b0 / T1907 / P10b0, all have a human subject with a different complement:

- **[T11b0]** N0VN1PREPN2 + N0Hum + VT + N1Hum + N2Abst + N2Vinf + PREP = “de”

  Ex*: La mère accuse son enfant de courir*. ‘The mother accuses her child of running’.

- **[P10B0]** = N0seVPREPN1 + N0Hum + VP + N1Hum + N1Abst + N1Vinf + PREP =“de”

  Ex: *On s'accuse d'avoir menti*. ‘One reproaches oneself for having lied’.

- **[T1907]** = N0VN1 NHum + VT +N1Hum N1Abst + N1Conc

  Ex: *Le juge accuse le criminel*. ‘The judge accuses the criminal’.

For the development of a formal grammar capable of correctly recognizing and translating the sentences which contain the verb *accuser*, we have to add other electronic dictionary resources and dictionaries for the detection of lexical units. We used the electronic dictionaries already integrated into the NooJ platform, such as:

Before	Seq.	After
s'est-il exclamé. "On	nous accuse de parler/أدان	librement et même parfois un
président de l'Assemblée nationale,	qui accuse le président/أدان	de l'UMP de vouloir
"fils de Le Pen" et	l'avoir accusé d'antisémitisme/أدان	et d'homophobie. Monté sur
de la fondation. En somme,	la France accuse un certain/أدان	retard sur le marché international
du 24 mars 1999 qui fit 39 morts.	Il accuse sa hiérarchie d'avoir pris/لام	à la légère l'incendie
le nombre de meurtres qu'	elle l'accuse d'avoir commis/لام	. £<DATE="050304"> § <PAGE="article_400155"> RUBRIQUE : France
M. Bartolone ne décolère pas.	Il accuse la majorité/أدان	du PS d'"essayer de
à la radicalisation du mouvement,	des proviseurs accusent des adultes/أدان	- parents d'élèves, enseignants - et
le 28 mars contre Michel Rocher.	On l'accuse d'avoir favorisé un laboratoire/لام	vidéo, VDM, à Courbevoie, où
qui que ce soit. Quand	son mari l'accuse d'avoir mis le doigt/لام	dans les fesses de ses
Avec une telle argumentation, on	vous accuse de racisme/أدان	et de nationalisme. Comment réagissez
veut tuer son chien, on	l'accuse de la rage/أدان	", fait remarquer, avant toute chose
jeunes Sénégalais de 20 à 25 ans	qui accusent le prêtre/أدان	sont d'anciens prostitués, prêts
premier secrétaire du PS a-	t-il accusé le gouvernement/أدان	, vendredi 12 août, de " laisser les
son éthique personnelle et qu'	on l'accuse d'avoir agi/لام	contre l'intérêt des actionnaires
positionnement de M. Henno qu'	il accuse d'avoir/أدان	" fait une campagne d'extrême
le rappeur Monsieur R. qu'	ils accusent d'incitation/أدان	à la haine pour son
'influence, je dis non. Si	vous m'accusez d'avoir monté un service/لام	parallèle qui n'était pas
des faits de maltraitance dont	ils accusaient leurs parents/أدان	. Les six accusés du procès
William Bourdon. Huit citoyens birmans,	qui accusaient l'entreprise/أدان	de travail forcé, ont retiré
de l'état d'urgence,	il accusait la gauche/أدان	d'être " à l'unisson
Politique - Société TITRE : Les témoignages	qui accusent l'armée/أدان	française au Rwanda Cinq hommes
refuge pour les survivants tutsis.	Les témoins accusent les militaires d'avoir facilité les enlèvements/لام	de Tutsis par les milices
TITRE : Au procès Matra-Thomson,	la défense accuse le plaignant d'avoir usurpé son titre/لام	de victime LE PROCÈS ouvert
la nation entre 1997 et 2002 " et	l'accuse d'avoir creusé la dette/لام	de " 300 milliards d'euros " alors
d'entrée des migrants malades.	L'association accuse le ministre/أدان	de l'intérieur d'avoir

Figure 4: Extraction from the corpus Le Monde and translation of the verb accuser into Arabic

- The delaf.nod which contains all the inflected forms of the single words corresponding to the lexical entries of the DELAS (Silberztein 1993);

- *Le DM* dictionary of French words (Trouilleux, 2011). This linguistic resource is integrated into the NooJ platform and itcontains 67,997 entries composed of determiners, pronouns, prepositions, conjunctions, numerals, adverbs, nouns, interjections, adjectives and verbs.

The grammar we have constructed must know all possible constructions without any ambiguity. For this reason, we chose to create for each syntactic construct its path independently of the other constructions to remove all the ambiguities using the precise semantic traits (concrete, abstract, human etc.) of each argument.

5 Automatic translation and generation of verbal predicates into Arabic

The automatic translation process is applied to the communication predicates obtained after the analysis and recognition phases.

We have already tried to implement our process of analysis and recognition of syntactic patterns on a newspaper corpus of *Le Monde*. We obtained results where the patterns and verbs found are disambiguated and annotated simply by the appropriate syntactic constructions (Figure 4).

We can see that the formal grammars allowed us not only to automatically recognize the different constructions, but also to translate the verb automatically into Arabic. However, our system not only allows us to translate a single verb but also the entire sentence.

Therefore, we added the grammars of translation (vAR) to each formal grammar. And we obtained the translation into Arabic of the different sentences that contain the verb *accuser* in its various constructions:

- Translation of *accuser*+**T11b0**+AR= لام (Lāma) 'To reproach'

  Ex: *La mère accuse son enfant de courir.*

  ➔ الأم تلوم ابنها على الركض

- Translation of accuser+**P10b0**+AR = لام (Lāma)

  Ex: *On s'accuse de mentir.*

  ➔ نلوم أنفسنا على الكذب

- Translation of accuser+**T1907**+AR= أدان (adāna) 'to accuse'

  Ex: *Le juge accuse le criminel.*

  ➔ أدان المجرم القاضي

Our system has succeeded in automatically translating the sentences into Arabic taking into account the meaning of the verb which varies according to the construction.

The software has thus made it possible to generate sentences naturally into Arabic without syntactic and semantic ambiguities.

The naturalness of the generated text is due to an automatic semantic syntactic analysis of open corpus, based on a broad description of the vocabulary. Our example adds to the examples of Silberztein (2015, 2016) to confirm that NooJ brings a significant qualitative leap for text generation.

6 Conclusion

We tried in this contribution to formalize the verb *accuser* as an example of verbs of speech, and to integrate it into the NooJ software. Thanks to the linguistic richness of the LVF verbal entries which helps the computer tools make a syntactic, semantic and morphological analysis of the verbs, we succeeded in automatically recognizing, extracting, and processing cases of *accuser* in a corpus of considerable size, the newspaper *Le Monde*.

This formalization was needed in order to obtain a reliable automatic translation. Thus, we created formal grammars to remove the ambiguity of the syntactic construct, since the meaning of the verb depends on the type of subject and the complement (human, concrete, abstract, etc.).

These grammars have led to the automatic recognition of syntactic constructions, which in turn removes ambiguities and generates sentences into Arabic taking into account the meaning of the verb in its original French context.

References

Jean-Paul Boons, Alain Guillet and Christian Leclère. 1976. *La structure des phrases simples en français. Constructions intransitives.* Genève : Droz.

Jean Dubois. 1979. *Dictionnaire de français langue étrangère*. Niveau II. Paris: Larousse.

Jean Dubois, Françoise Dubois-Charlier. 1997. *Les Verbes Français*. Paris: Larousse-Bordas (diffuseur exclusif).

John W. Hutchins.2001. Machine Translation over fifty years. *Histoire épistémologique du langage.* Volume 23 Numéro 1 pp 7-31

Jacqueline Léon. 1998. Les débuts de la traduction automatique en France (1959- 1968): à contretemps?, *Modèles Linguistiques*, tome XIX, fascicule 2, pp 55-86.

Max Silberztein. 2003. *NooJ Manual.* Available at: www.nooj4nlp.net

Max Silberztein. 2015. *La formalisation des langues: l'approache de NooJ.* ISTE Editions, London,UK.

Max Silberztein. 2016. *Formalizing Natural Languages: The NooJ Approach.* Wiley ISTE, London,UK.

François Trouilleux. 2011. *Le DM*, A French dictionary for NooJ. In *Automatic Processing of Various Levels of Linguistic Phenomena: Selected Papers from the NooJ 2011 International Conference* (eds. K. Vučković, B. Bekavac and M. Silberztein). Cambridge Scholars Publishing, pp 16-28.

Using Serious Games to Correct French Dictations: Proposal for a New Unity3D/NooJ Connector

Ikram Bououd and Rania Fafi
Higher Institute of Management of Gabes
ikram.bououd@gmail.com, ranyafafi93@gmail.com

Abstract

The remarkable growth in serious games use has gradually pushed them to be present in every single domain. However, in language learning we did not find any reliable games developed for dictation exercises, commonly used for the teaching of French. This involves natural language processing in the form of an interactive game that can automatically generate corrections and assess game users. In order to fill this research gap, we propose to take advantage of the assets provided by the NooJ platform and develop a game combining NooJ and the 3D game platform Unity3D.

1 Introduction

Serious Games (SG) constitute a new educational frame. This oxymoron represents a powerful means to spread serious content in an entertaining way (Abt, 1970). SG are experiencing a huge increase within our societies and invading every single domain: healthcare, the military, education, advertisement, coaching, etc. (Alvarez and Rostaing, 2014). The important use of these games has gradually put them as an important research area, especially when SG are dealing with an attractive and crucial topic such as education and language learning.

Developing a serious game for language learning, in particular for a dictation exercise, led us to make use of different resources from Natural Language Processing (NLP). The main challenge was to create a successful connection between the game platform, here Unity3D, and the NLP platform, here NooJ. To the best of our knowledge such a connection between these two platforms has never been proposed.

This game allows better interactivity along with automatic correction of a French dictation exercise for the language learner. This will offer added value to language learning and can make the gamer more sophisticated.

2 Serious Games

Alvarez defines SG as "computer applications having as original intention to combine both serious aspects (serious), with fun aspects from video games (game). Such an association is achieved by providing a learning scenario corresponding, from a programming point of view, to implement a decor (sound and graphics), story and suitable rules; therefore it moves away from restricting the game to entertainment" (Alvarez and Rostaing, 2014).

Indeed, SG are entertaining games for educational purpose. The main objective is to exploit the entertaining aspect of video games to facilitate learning concepts, traditionally taught through conventional teaching methods. The range of usage areas of SG is very wide such as scientific exploration, medicine and education. More precisely, the educational aspect of SG is one of their greatest assets. Indeed, SG are promoting and opening new horizons for active learning and provide a learning-by-doing experience. Thanks to their graphics and design, SG are well accepted among the young generation since they succeed in keeping them concentrated on their tasks and engage them in the learning process (Berta et al., 2016).

The learning part of the game is the most important. Many discussions have explored reward systems as ways to motivate student participation and practice. However, when people began to look at the potential of games for student engagement, they found that the games fit well within the theories of learning.

This approach can potentially help students master the learning process. The use of online gaming integrated into education has a positive impact on student learning thanks to their graphics and design, since SG keep them concentrated on their tasks and

Proceedings of the Linguistic Resources for Automatic Natural Language Generation Workshop, pages 49–52, Santiago de Compostela, Spain, September 4, 2017.

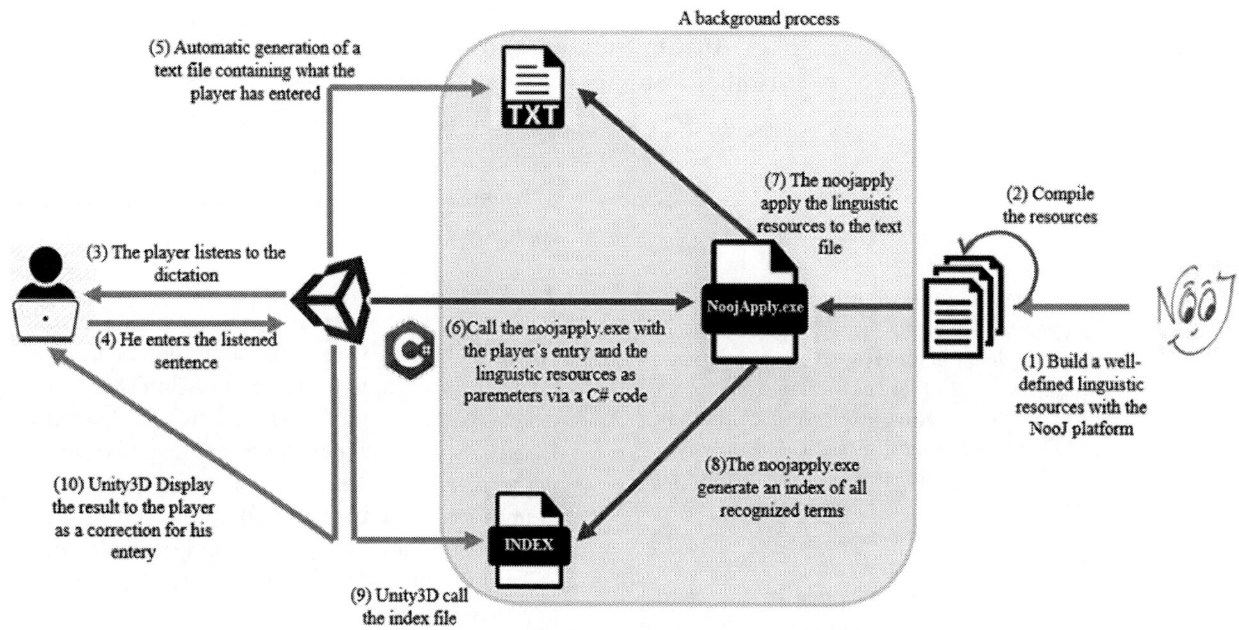

Figure 1: Approach overview

engage them in the learning process (Berta et al., 2016).

3 Learning languages and games

Learning languages is crucial and requires several competencies: listening, speaking, pronunciation, reading, writing, as well as dictation, which combines listening and writing. Language learning requires concentration and endurance, which are hard to maintain for a long periods of time. Consequently, learners will quickly feel bored, lose concentration and then neglect the engagement to learn.

Games overcome this point by integrating heavy learning materials in a playful way and make learning processing smooth and encouraging (Graesser, 2016). The literature of serious games provides several games for language learning such as English pronunciation (Trooster et al., 2016) or German learning (Alyaz et al., 2017). Some games are proposed for children with Down syndrome (Simao et al., 2016) to learn phonetics, etc. Existing games did not provide an automatic language processing of users' input and did not correct their responses with a customized way. Indeed, they need to write down their responses and compare them later with the right responses provided by the game (Alyaz et al., 2017).

We decided to take advantage of the NooJ platform to create an automatic language-learning process that reinforces dictation and writing skills. To the best of our knowledge, a game dealing with interactive correction of dictation has not yet been proposed.

4 SG Proposal based on NLP

4.1 NooJ/Unity connection: Approach overview

Building the connection between Unity3D and NooJ was the first step we took (Figure 1). Dictation is designed to build various language skills - listening, pronunciation, spelling and writing words correctly from individual letters. First of all, we concentrated on building new NooJ resources (dictionaries and grammars) to recognize certain word forms from their components (prefixes, affixes and suffixes) (Silberztein, 2003). This task allows us to determine whether each word entered by the player is written correctly or not.

But this is not enough for dictation correction or detecting the incorrect agreement between subject and verb or any mistaken combinations in the sentence. So we have resorted to building another syntactic grammar that describes full sentences, and decides whether the formulated sentences are consistent in terms of agreement, gender, number and person or not.

Secondly, after building the linguistic resources, we moved on to compile them to be used as parameters in the command-line noojapply within NooJ (Silberztein and Tutin, 2005).

When the player listens to the provided dictation, he/she enters his/her response in a text box inside the game. After sending his/her response, Unity3D (using C# code) will divide the entered sentence into separate words in a new generated text file; each of these words would be a NooJ platform entry to be processed.

Noojapply is then called from the C# code inside the game. At this point, we are able to connect the entry of the player, saved automatically to a text file, to the compiled lexical resources, the parameters that noojapply needs.

NooJ then applies the provided linguistic resources word by word in a loop to detect eventual misspelled words and sends the index of each word to Unity3D to be saved in an index file. And then it will apply syntactic resources to detect any wrong agreement within the sentence.

The coherent answer is the one that matches one of the grammars' paths. This index file is what we use to display the correction to the player. The final result is displayed to the player as a correction to his/her mistakes.

4.2 Experimentation

The player explores the terrain searching for a sound source, once he/she finds it; he/she will be able to control the listening with a keyboard key.

When the player finishes listening to the French dictation, a new panel appears, giving him a place to write the sentence heard (Figure 2).

Figure 2: The entry field

After writing the sentence heard and by clicking on the "Envoyer" button (Figure 3) the correction process begins in the game's background.

Figure 3: The entry field after listening to the message

Some examples of detected mistakes and their corrections can be seen in Figure 4 and Figure 5.

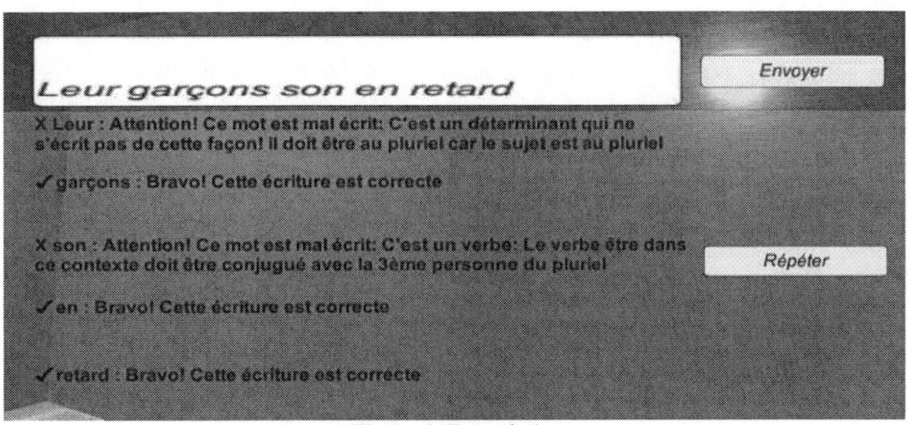

Figure 4: Example 1

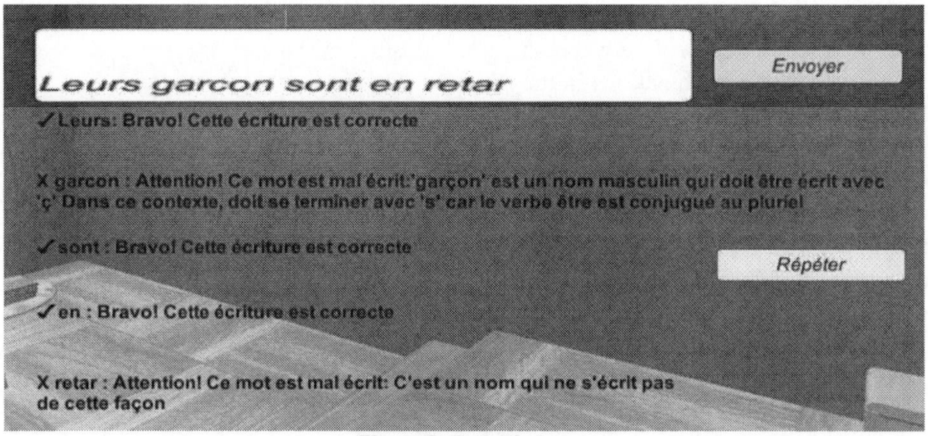

Figure 5: Example 2

5 Conclusion

Serious games are powerful educational tools that can achieve pedagogical goals and engage players in deep learning. However, they need strong support from NLP platforms, such as NooJ, in order to be able to perform automatic dictation tasks and correct players' answers. This paper is a proposal for the creation of a connection between NooJ and Unity3D. This connection will open horizons to several future jobs mixing serious games and natural language processing.

References

Arthur C. Graesser 2016. Reflections on Serious Games. Book chapter from *Instructional Techniques to Facilitate Learning and Motivation of Serious Games*, pp 199-212.

Clark C. Abt 1970. *Serious Games*. Viking Press.

Julian Alvarez and Aurélia Rostaing 2014. *Autour des jeux sérieux (serious games): Définition générale et terminologie*. PowerPoint Presentation. Bibliothèque Nationale de France, Paris. `http://www.ludoscience.com/FR/diffusion/893-Autour-des-jeux-serieux-serious-games--Definition-generale-et-terminologie.html`. Date Accessed: May 12, 2017.

José Simao, Louisa Cotrim, Teresa Condeco, Tiago Cardoso, Miguel Palha, Yves Rybarczyk and José Barata. 2016. Using games for the phonetics awareness for children with Down Syndrome. *Serious Games, Interaction and Simulation: 6th International Conference SGAMES* 2016 Porto Portugal, (eds. C. Vaz de Carvalho, P. Escudeiro, A. Coelho), Springer International Publishing, pp 1-8

Max Silberztein. 2003. *NooJ Manual* Available for download at: `www.nooj4nlp.net`.

Max Silberztein and Agnès Tutin. 2005. NooJ, un outil TAL pour l'enseignement des langues. *Application pour l'étude de la morphologie lexicale en FLE*. Special Atala, 8(2), pp 123-134.

Riccardo Berta, Francesco Bellotti, Erik van der Spek and Thomas Winkler. 2016. A Tangible Serious Game Approach to Science, Technology, Engineering, and Mathematics (STEM) Education. *Handbook of Digital Games and Entertainment Technologies*, pp 571-592.

Wim Trooster, Sui Lin Goei, Anouk Ticheloven, Esther Oprins, Gillian van de Boer-Visschedijk, Gemma Corbalan and Martin Van Schaik. 2016. The Effectiveness of the Game LINGO Online: A Serious Game for English Pronunciation. In *Simulation and Serious Games for Education*, pp 125-136.

Yunus Alyaz, Dorothea Spaniel-Weise and Esim Gursoy. 2017, A Study on Using Serious Games in Teaching German as a Foreign Language. *Journal of Education and Learning* 6(3), pp 250-264.

Association for Computational Linguistics
209 N. Eighth Street
Stroudsburg, Pennsylvania 18360

ISBN 978-1-5108-4758-3

9 781510 847583

CURRAN ASSOCIATES INC.
proceedings.com